Psychology
Student Edition

Written by: Rebecca Stark

Educational Impressions

The purchase of this book entitles
the buyer to exclusive reproduction
rights. Permission to reproduce
these pages is extended to the
purchaser only.

Cover Design and Illustrations by Nelsy Fontalvo

*Explanation of cover design: This is an example of the type of ambigious figure used by psychologists in their experiments in the field of visual perception. This particular one was devised by psychologist Edward Boring. He named it "my wife and my mother-in-law." There are two alternative modes of perceiving it: as an attractive young girl with her head turned from the viewer and as a witch-like old lady with her head buried in her wrap. The same set of physical lines striking the retina gives rise to two distinctive perceptual images. Once both modes have been recognized, the perceiver can easily identify each.

Teacher Edition ISBN: 0-910857-37-7
Student Edition ISBN: 0-910857-38-5

Copyright © Educational Impressions, 1986

EDUCATIONAL IMPRESSIONS, INC.
Hawthorne, New Jersey 07507

Table of Contents

What Is Psychology?..5
Human Development...5
    Heredity and Environment..5-6
    Growth and Development..7-8
The Nervous System...9-14
    The Neuron...9-10
    The Peripheral Nervous System..10
    The Brain...11-14
Cognitive Development..15-16
Creative Problem Solving...17-19
Intelligence..20
Sensation and Perception...21-24
Conditioning, Learning and Memory..25-26
    Classic Conditioning...25
    Instrumental Learning...27-29
    Memory..30-31
Motivation and Emotion...32-34
Altered States of Consciousness..35-36
Frustration and Conflict...37-38
Mental Disorders...39-40
Psychotherapy...41
Personality..45-47
Theories of Personality..48-56
Social Psychology..57-64
    Social Attitudes..58-61
    Social Groups...62-64

What Is Psychology?

From the beginnings of civilization, human beings have striven to "know themselves." Psychology is an attempt to do just that! It is the science of mental processes and behavior.

Modern psychology comprises many subject areas: sensation - perception, motivation, emotion, innate patterns (those possessed at birth), learning, thinking, intelligence, personality, group dynamics and behavior pathology. The sub-branch known as physiological psychology emphasizes the physiological variables which affect behavior and mental processes. Like in other sciences, research in psychology is observational and experimental and is done both in the field and in the laboratory. Psychologists analyze the data they obtain by statistical methods. Of course, there are obvious limits to the types and amount of experimentation which can be ethically performed. Psychologists differ in their research methods and clinical techniques. These differences are dependent upon their theoretical and philosophical views. For example, some psychologists show a preference for the psychoanalytic therapies set forth by Sigmund Freud; they focus on the early, mostly unconscious, developmental origins of personality. Others, known as behaviorists, focus upon overt, observable behavior; their theories are based upon the principles of conditioning and adaptive behavior.

Psychology has matured through the centuries from its beginnings in supernatural beliefs, magic and taboo to its development as a scientific discipline. In fact, it has become so broad, that it has become essential for psychologists to specialize in one of the numerous and varied fields. Each in his or her way attempts to help people "know themselves"!

Human Development

Heredity and Environment

For many years psychologists argued whether human behavior tendencies were caused by a person's heredity or environment. It became known as the nature-nurture controversy. Today we no longer speak of heredity <u>versus</u> environment. Although some psychologists place more or less stress on one or the other, it is generally agreed that heredity and environment interact to contribute to the making of distinct individuals. Your genes do set limits upon your physical and intellectual development; however, your environment determines how you develop within those limits.

1. It is usually difficult to determine the importance of heredity upon an individual's intelligence. The presence of "trisomy-21" is an exception. Explain what is meant by "trisomy-21." (C)

_____

_____

_____

The field of behavior genetics investigates the relation of genetic potential to expressed behavior. The first major experiments in this area were carried out by R.C. Tryon. The purpose of his experiments, first begun in 1927, was to establish two strains of rats: one of bright maze-learners and one of dull maze-learners. By selective breeding he accomplished what he had set out to do. Selective breeding is the technique of mating animals that display certain traits. This is continued for a number of generations. From each generation only those displaying the trait are bred. Tryon's results were as he had expected. The bright maze-learners produced bright offspring and the dull maze-learners produced dull offspring.

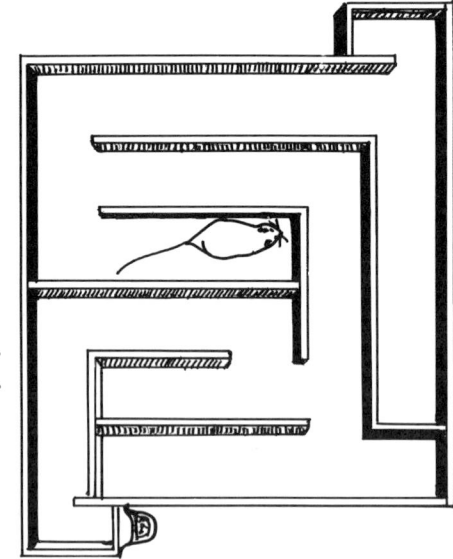

2. Other scientists have corroborated Tryon's results. What general conclusion can be made based upon these studies? (C,AN)

___

___

Families often show similarities in abilities and behaviors. We can not jump to the conclusion, however, that these similarities are entirely due to heredity, for families also share similar environments.

3. Compare and contrast fraternal and identical twins. Evaluate the importance of identical twins in the study of human behavior. (C,AN,E)

___

___

___

Most people have 23 pairs of chromosomes. The 23rd pair of chromosomes determines the person's sex: xx for a woman and xy for a man. Some males, however, have an extra y in the sex chromosome. These males have an unusually tall stature. Some studies have shown that there is a greater than average number of xyy males among prisoners. They also find that these xyy males exhibit violent and aggressive behavior. Some scientists believe that the aggressive behavior may be directly attributed to their genetic abnormality. Others argue that it is due to the way people react to their large size.

4. There have been cases in which xyy persons who have been accused of crimes have asked for pardon based upon their genetic abnormality. Choose a point of view and compose your opening remarks as the public defender or prosecutor. (C,AN,S,E)

Growth and Development

Human beings gradually develop. Although a person's genetic makeup is established at conception, the physical and behavioral traits that will express themselves do not become apparent for some time. In general, a child's body develops from head to foot and from near to far. In other words, the muscles that control the movement of head and neck should mature before those needed for crawling or walking. Shoulder and hip muscles will develop earlier than those in the fingers and toes.

The rate at which children develop varies - partly because of their environments and partly because of their different genetic makeup. Studies seem to indicate that a child cannot learn motor skills until the appropriate muscles are mature, even if the child is encouraged to practice. For example, Arnold Gesell, in his study of identical twins, encouraged one twin to practice skills, such as stair-climbing, while the other twin remained in a playpen. As soon as the twin who had been practicing mastered the skill, the other twin was given the opportunity to try. In most cases the "control" twin performed the task about as well as the first. There have been a few exceptions to these findings, however. Children more easily learn tasks which require special skills, such as swimming or skating, if they are given guidance and practice. Also, infants who are allowed the freedom to explore their environments seem to develop into more active and outgoing children.

Sensorimotor Development

- 4 weeks - control of eye movements; ability to follow an object visually, and so forth
- 16 weeks - ability to balance head
- 28 weeks - ability to use the hands for grasping and manipulating objects
- 40 weeks - control of the trunk, enabling the child to sit and crawl
- 52 weeks - control of the legs and feet, enabling the child to stand and walk about

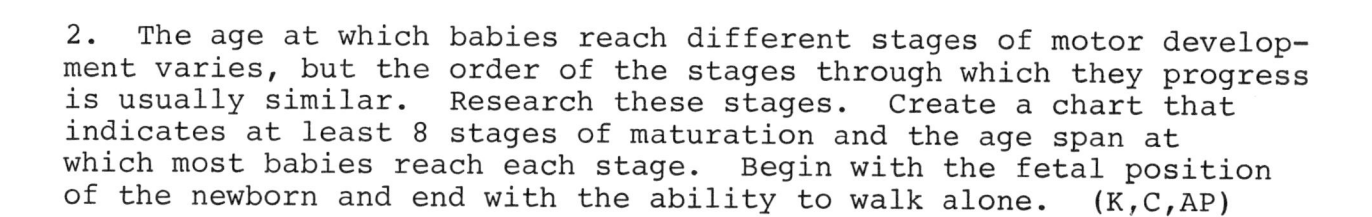

1. Analyze the reasons children usually develop from head to foot and from near to far. (C,AN)

_____

_____

2. The age at which babies reach different stages of motor development varies, but the order of the stages through which they progress is usually similar. Research these stages. Create a chart that indicates at least 8 stages of maturation and the age span at which most babies reach each stage. Begin with the fetal position of the newborn and end with the ability to walk alone. (K,C,AP)

Critical Periods

Some psychologists believe that the best time for a child to learn a skill is when his or her body is just mature enough to master that skill. They feel that if it is too early or too late, the child will not master it. Extensive research with animals has been done which supports the "critical-period hypothesis."

3. Find out what is meant by imprinting and analyze its relation to the critical-period hypothesis. (C,AN)

_____

_____

_____

4. Draw a humorous picture that illustrates imprinting in ducks or geese that have been hatched away from their mothers. (C,AP)

5. Although its imprinting urge remains strong, if a gosling is kept in the dark for 2 or 3 days after hatching, imprinting does not usually occur. This is due to the development of another innate urge. Speculate as to what this urge is. (C,AN)

_____

_____

Adolescence

Adolescence, the period of growth and development that comes between childhood and adulthood, is one of change - both physiological and psychological. The ages at which the physical changes take place vary, but, in general, girls develop about two years earlier than boys. The psychological changes that occur vary from culture to culture. A 17-year-old might be considered an adolescent in one culture and an adult in another.

6. Even within a country sub-cultures and socioeconomic groups vary as to when they regard an adolescent as having become an adult. At what age will you be (or were you) considered an adult? Usually a transition rite is held to mark the passing from one status to the next. Draw a picture to show how your change in status was (or will be) marked. (C,AP)

Adulthood

Many psychologists believe that personality is formed during childhood and adolescence. Some, however, take the view that an individual continues to develop and change throughout adulthood.

7. Researchers have studied the effects of social and environmental events upon adult personality development and change. Create a poster that depicts events which occur during adulthood which might have an impact on an adult's personality. (K,C,AN)

The Nervous System

Our nervous system, like that of other vertebrates, includes our brain, spinal cord and nerves. Its main functions are to receive input in the form of stimuli, to process and store the effects of the stimuli, and to generate output based upon those effects in the form of behavior.

The nervous system is divided into three main sub-systems. The central nervous system consists of the brain, the spinal cord, and their associated blood vessels, fluids and membranes. The peripheral nervous system is made up of the cranial (pertaining to the skull) nerves, the spinal nerves and the part of the autonomic, or involuntary, nervous system that is outside the brain and spinal cord. The autonomic nervous system controls such involuntary activities as breathing, heart rate and digestion.

The structure of both the central nervous system and the peripheral nervous system consists of neurons, or nerve cells, surrounded by supporting cells. An individual is born with more than 15 billion neurons. These are the basic units of the nervous system. Each has contact with other neurons and together they integrate, conduct and transmit coded information in the form of electrical impulses.

The Neuron (Nerve Cell)

Neurons vary in shape, size and type of activity. Some, such as those in the brain, are only a fraction of an inch; others, such as those extending from the big toe into the central nervous system, reach several feet. They all share certain common features, however. Every neuron has a nucleus which contains the genetic information of the cell. The nucleus is enclosed in the soma, or cell body, where most of the chemical reactions involved in the cell's life processes take place. The outer covering of the cell is the cell membrane. The chemicals must pass through the membrane before a reaction can occur.

Most neurons have 2 kinds of processes, or extensions: dendrites and axons. These processes make it possible for one neuron to stimulate another. The dendrites are short, thread-like processes with small, spiny projections. They make up the major part of the area known as the dendritic zone. This dendritic zone is the area most receptive to stimulation. The axon is a long, thin process. The end of each axon branches into small fibers, called axon terminals. These terminals come close to the dendritic zone of other neurons. Covering most axons is a white, fatty material called a myelin sheath. The dendrites transmit impulses toward the cell body and the axons conduct the impulses away from the cell body.

The area in which an axon terminal of one neuron comes close to the dendritic zone of another is called a synapse. The synapse is filled with fluid containing many chemicals. When transmitter chemicals released by the axon terminals of one neuron cross the synapse, they stimulate the dendrites and cell body of another neuron. Because the axon is relatively long, it is possible for a neuron to stimulate a neuron some distance away. Activity in one neuron may affect activity in many other cells in many parts of the body.

The Neuron

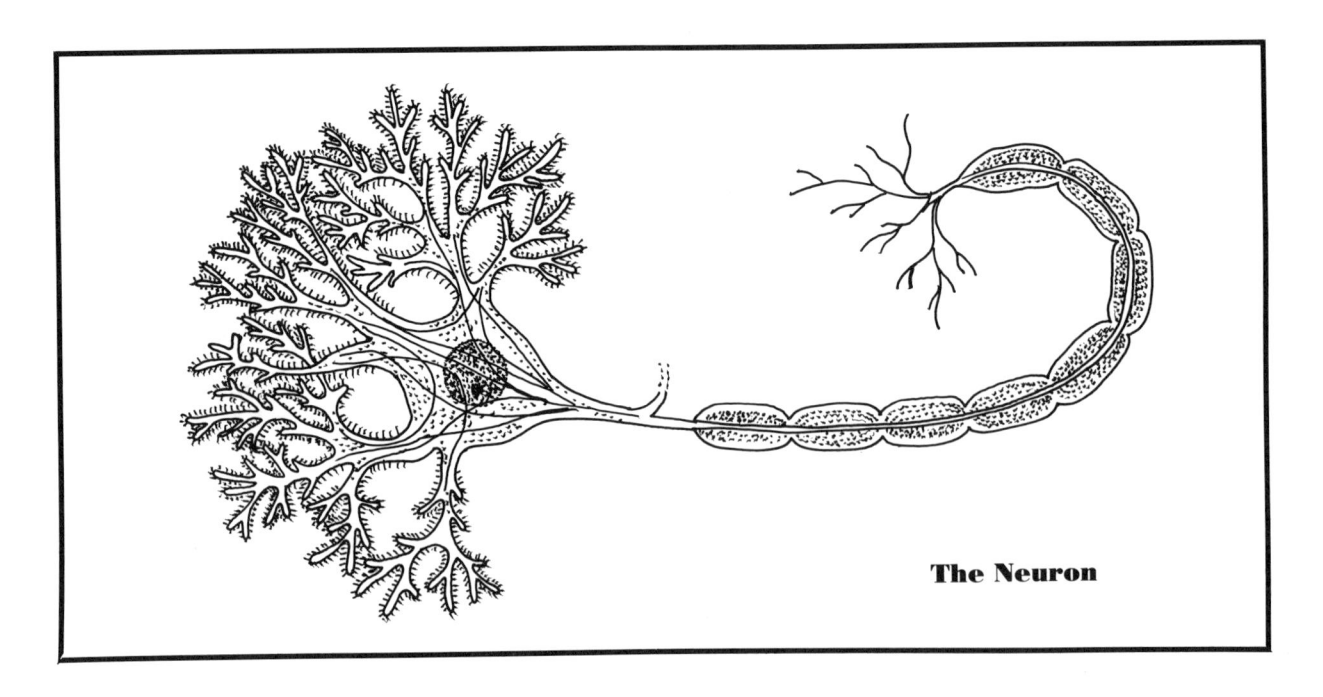

1. Label the parts of a neuron on the diagram: nucleus, cell body, dendrites, dendritic spines, axon, and axon terminals. (K,AP)

2. Explain the difference between sensory and motor neurons. (K,C)

_____

_____

3. A synapse can be excitatory or inhabitory. Find out what these terms mean. Draw a diagram that explains this phenomenon. (C,AP)

The Peripheral Nervous System

A bundle of axons running together is a nerve. <u>Spinal nerves</u> run in pairs up and down the spinal cord, one on each side. They carry impulses from most areas of the skin, the internal organs and the joints. The impulses go through the spinal cord into the brain. Then they carry motor impulses back to the muscles and glands involved. There are 31 pairs of spinal nerves.

Cranial nerves arise in pairs from the brainstem. They are mostly concerned with the skin, muscles, etc. of the facial area and with the special senses, such as olfactory, optic and acoustic. There are 12 pairs of cranial nerves.

1. In order to excite a nerve fibre and to initiate an action potential, the stimulus to the fibre must be of a certain strength. This strength is called the threshold. This is often called the all-or-none law. Explain why. (C,AP,AN)

_____

_____

_____

The Brain

Your brain probably weighs about 3 pounds, or 1.3 kilograms, but they are the most important 3 pounds in your body! In the embryonic stage the human brain has 3 main divisions: the forebrain, the midbrain and the hindbrain. The adult brain, however, is divided into 5 major sections: (1) the cerebrum, (2) the thalamus and hypothalamus, (3) the medulla, (4) the pons and cerebellum, and (5) the midbrain. The cerebrum, thalamus and hypothalamus develop from the forebrain. The pons, cerebellum and medulla develop from the hindbrain.

The folded surface layer of the brain is called the cortex. The cerebral cortex comprises the folded surface area of the cerebrum and the cerebellar cortex comprises the surface area of the cerebellum. The cortex is where most of the neurons, or nerve cells, are concentrated. It is believed that an individual is born with about 10 billion or more neurons in the cortex, but that at about age 20 some begin to atrophy, or deteriorate. By about 75 years of age, the weight of the brain decreases about 10 percent.

The cerebrum, the largest part of the human brain, is where most of your important mental functions take place. It is divided into two symmetrical, protruding pouches, which are called the left and right hemispheres. Because of the crossing of nerve fibres, the left half of the brain controls the right side of the body and vice versa. Each hemisphere is covered with a gray mantle - the cerebral cortex; it is about 1/10 of an inch, or about 1/4 of a centimeter, thick. Deep within each cerebral hemisphere, beneath the cortex, are large masses of gray matter composed of nerve-cell bodies. These structures, known collectively as the basal ganglia, help control motor responses. Much of the interior of the hemispheres is made up of white matter, or tissue, consisting mostly of nerve fibers.

The hemispheres are connected by tracts of nerve fibres called commissures. The largest commissure is the corpus callosum. If the commissures became damaged, one side of the brain would not know what the other side is doing.

The thalamus, located between the cerebral hemispheres, is a large egg-shaped mass of gray matter. Its main function seems to be that of a central receiving station for incoming sensory messages (with the exception of the olfactory system). It receives this input from the sensory nerves and sends impulses to the cortex, where the sensory areas are located.

The hypothalamus is a small structure which lies below the thalamus. It regulates body temperature, some metabolic processes and other autonomic (involuntary) activities. Studies indicate that the hypothalamus is involved in the control of emotion and motivation.

The medulla oblongata comprises the nervous tissue at the bottom of the brain. Respiration, circulation and other bodily functions are controlled by the medulla.

The cerebellum and pons make up the hindbrain. The cerebellum, which has a cortex somewhat similar to that of the cerebrum, is responsible for the regulation and coordination of complex muscular movement. The pons contains many nuclei. Some of them serve as tracts which connect the cerebellum with the cerebrum. Others help control sleep and waking.

The midbrain connects the cerebellum and pons with the cerebrum. Included in the midbrain is much of the reticular formation. The reticular formation helps control an individual's arousal level.

1. Find out the etymology (origin of a word or other linguistic form) of the word "cortex." Judge the appropriateness of the label.

_____

_____

2. Compare the organization of your brain with that of a large, corporate organization. Prepare a corporate chart showing the levels of hierarchy and the delegation of authority. (C,AP,AN,S,E)

3. In the embryonic stage, the brain has three major divisions. Draw a chart to show from which major division each part of the brain developed: cerebrum, thalamus, hypothalamus, cerebellum, pons, and medulla. (K,C,AP)

4. Find out which of the brain structures are collectively known as the brainstem. Draw a diagram and label. (K,C,AP)

The Cerebral Hemispheres

Although the cerebral hemispheres are mirror images of each other, there are important differences between them. If you are right-handed, as about 90% of the world's population is, then your left hemisphere is probably the dominant one. The dominant hemisphere controls such activities as speech. The non-dominant hemisphere is sometimes called the "perceptual" or "emotional" hemisphere. Although it understands language, it seldom talks or writes. If you are left-handed, we can't be certain which half of your cerebrum is dominant! It would seem that your right hemisphere should be dominant, but this isn't always the case! In some left-handers, both hemispheres seem to share the ability to read and write, and neither is dominant. In others the left hemisphere seems to be dominant in spite of the left-handedness! Scientists don't really know why.

5. The inability to recognize the meaning of words or to speak in meaningful terms is known as "aphasia." It is caused by a cerebral lesion or other type of brain damage. On which side of the brain would this type of lesion most likely be found? Explain. (K,C)

_____

_____

6. In some types of brain damage the individual displays difficulties in the perception and retention of nonverbal stimuli, such as faces and melodies. On which side of the brain would a lesion that produces this disorder most likely be found? Explain. (K,C)

_____

_____

7. If a patient received a brain transplant, would the brain receive a new body, or would the body receive a new brain? (AN,E)

_____

_____

_____

Split-Brain Operations

In 1953 psychologists Roger Sperry and R.E. Meyers performed their first split-brain operation on a cat. They wanted to find out what would happen if the corpus callosum, the tissue that connects the two cerebral hemispheres, were cut. The split-brain procedure Sperry and Meyers performed involved cutting the cat's corpus callosum and splitting its optic nerve. The result of such an operation is 2 mostly separate brains. Input that is seen by the right eye is recorded by the right hemisphere only. Input seen by the left eye is recorded only in the left hemisphere.

Once the cat recovered from the procedure, it was tested. They blindfolded one eye and trained the cat to solve a visual problem. Then they blindfolded the other eye and tested the untrained eye. The cat acted unfamiliar with the problem and could even be taught to respond in an opposite manner. For example, the cat might be taught to choose a cube if the right eye receives the input and a ball if the left eye receives it.

Although you might think that split-brain operations would never be performed upon humans, that is not so. They have been performed on patients who suffer from severe epileptic attacks. Epilepsy is caused by damaged nerve cells. If the damage is in the input or processing areas of the brain, the individual suffers little more than short lapses in consciousness; however, when the damaged neurons are in the output areas, the condition becomes more severe. Motor seizures involve sudden contraction of muscles, loss of consciousness, and twitching or jerking of the arms and legs. Even severe forms, called "grand mal," last only a few minutes and are followed by little memory of what occurred.

Epilepsy is usually caused by damage to a specific area on one side of the brain; nevertheless, an EEG (electroencephalograph) record would show spikes on both sides of the brain. These spikes represent large bursts of electrical activity and usually are symptoms of brain damage. In this case, however, the spike responses come from tissue that seems to be healthy. The reason stems from the fact that each hemisphere is a mirror image of the other.

The cells in the area of the damage cause increased electrical activity. They send an "excited message" to the mirror-image cells in the other hemisphere. The mirror-image cells then fire a similar electrical message back to the area of damage, and so on. Each time the message flashes back and forth, a few more cells get fired up. If enough cells become involved, a grand mal attack occurs.

The first known split-brain operation was performed on an American soldier who had been taken prisoner during the Korean War. While in the prison camp, he was severely beaten on the head with the butt of a rifle. He began to have epileptic seizures. By the time he was released, his condition was so severe that he was having about 12 or more grand mal attacks each day. His doctors believed he would either die or commit suicide, as many others with such severe cases of the disorder had done. They decided to cut his corpus callosum.

The seizures stopped almost immediately. Although he could communicate fairly normally, however, he seemed to have two separate minds. Because he was right-handed, his left hemisphere, the "talking" hemisphere, was dominant and controlled his right hand and leg. His left hand, however, often caused him great embarrassment, for it did things for which he could give no rational (verbal) reason, usually in emotional situations!

Since then other patients with extremely severe cases of epilepsy have had similar operations. In some of the patients, the dominant hemisphere took control of both sides of the body. In the majority of cases the two hemispheres learned to share control, although the dominant one usually had control. In a few cases, however, neither hemisphere was able to take control enough to coordinate all bodily movements.

8. In split-brain operations performed on epileptics only the corpus callosum is cut. The optic nerve is left intact. Analyze the reasons for performing this type of surgery to relieve epileptic symptoms. Judge the ethics of performing this type of operation on human subjects. (C,AN,E)

_____

_____

_____

9. If a person whose corpus callosum has been cut receives a brief stimulus in his left visual field only, he will say that he has seen nothing. Analyze the reason for this and devise a way in which the right hemisphere might "tell" what it has seen. (C,AN)

_____

_____

_____

Cognitive Development: The Development of Thinking

Cognitive processes are those that go beyond sensing and perceiving. They involve the formation of ideas! For centuries philosophers have speculated about the manner in which the human mind develops. Today there are still many questions which cognitive psychologists discuss, often with a great deal of disagreement: Are infants born with an innate ability to think and process language? Which is more important to the development of intelligence: a child's genetic blueprint or the social environment in which he is placed? Do all children pass through the same stages of development or are these stages the result of cultural influences? How important is the rate of development?

Jean Piaget

One of the most highly respected and influential scientists to focus on cognitive development was the Swiss psychologist Jean Piaget (1896-1980). Piaget based his theory on three general principles: organization, equilibrium and adaptation. He believed that every infant is born with innate mental functions, which he called schemata. The simplest schemata are the sensorimotor reflexes, but the schemata constantly interrelate. This mental function that guides the schemata to create complex mental structures out of simple ones is called <u>organization</u>. For example, an infant learns the individual simple percepts of how his mother looks, feels and sounds and then integrates them into the complex schema of "mother." Piaget believed that humans have an innate desire that motivates us to increase the complexity of our schemata and behavior. He called this inner drive <u>equilibrium</u>.

Piaget also believed that humans have an innate tendency to adjust to the environment. He referred to the continuous interaction between an individual and the environment as <u>adaptation</u>. The two types of adaptation are assimilation and accomodation. In assimilation the individual takes into mental organization from the environment whatever can be incorporated into the existing schemata; he tends to perceive only what he can make sense of from previous knowledge even though some distortion may occur. When new stimuli are too strong to be ignored, accomodation takes place. If the input won't fit into the existing schemata, a new schema is formed or old ones are modified.

According to Piaget, cognitive development occurs in four major stages. Although we go from one stage to the next at different ages, the order never varies. The incorporation of the mental organization of each stage is necessary before one can proceed to the next. The first stage, which usually occurs in the first two years, is the <u>sensorimotor period</u> during which the infant begins with innate reflexes and action schemata. He gradually integrates his sense impressions into more complex schemata. The second stage, from about two to seven, is the <u>pre-operational</u> period during which the child learns to speak; his perception can be represented by words and he can see the world in symbolic terms. The third stage, from about seven to twelve, is the stage of <u>concrete operations</u>; the child learns to classify objects by similarities and differences. The child develops conservation abilities and realizes that certain properties of an object (such as length, quantity and weight) do not change despite changes in other perceivable features. The fourth and final stage begins at about age twelve and may continue into adulthood. In this stage of <u>formal operations</u> the individual reaches cognitive maturity. The individual's schemata, or mental structures, have become complex enough for him to think logically even with respect to abstract terms.

1. Create a poster that charts the 4 stages of cognitive development according to Piaget. Cite examples of the experiences that characterize each stage. Illustrate your poster with pictures you have drawn or cut out of magazines which show children in experiences characteristic of each stage. (C,AP,AN)

2. Experiments have shown that up to about age 6 most children are egocentric; they cannot see the world from perspectives other than their own. Cut out a picture of a scene and ask several children aged 5, 6, and 7 to describe how the scene would look from a different point of view. Report on your results. (C,AP,AN)

3. Conservation is an aspect of mental development in which the child understands that certain properties of an object do not change despite changes in other perceivable features of the object. Devise an experiment to test children's understanding of the principle of conservation of matter, volume and/or weight. Analyze the results of your experiment. (C,AP,N)

Jerome Bruner

The theory of cognitive development set forth by American psychologist Jerome Bruner (1915-) is similar to Piaget's; Bruner, however, is more concerned with the role of education and experience. According to his theory, we progress through three stages, each involving a different way of representing knowledge. Stage 1 is the <u>enactive mode of representation</u>, or the representation of knowledge by motor schemata. In this mode of representation, we learn by <u>doing</u> something with our muscles. The second stage is the <u>iconic mode of representation</u>. In this mode knowledge is represented in the form of images and percepts, such as the memory of someone's face. The third and most complex stage is the <u>symbolic mode</u> of representation. This stage involves the use of words and other symbols to represent abstract ideas as well as concrete ones. To Piaget the use of language was dependent upon the level of cognitive development. To Bruner the level of cognitive development was somewhat dependent upon the ability to use language.

4. The enactive mode is the principal way of representing knowledge for an infant or young child; however, it operates to some degree throughout our lives. Draw a picture of something you learned within in the last five years in the enactive mode. (C,AP)

"Aha!" Creative Problem Solving "Aha!"

Problem solving begins with the discovery that a problem exists. Once the individual recognizes, or perceives, the nature of the problem, he must decide how to solve it. Some problems can be solved by reproducing what was previously learned. Other problems, however, require solutions that are new and original for the individual. This type of productive thinking (as opposed to reproductive) is known as creative problem solving.

As we work on a problem, especially a difficult one, there are silent periods. During these lapses the individual doesn't seem to be working on the problem, and yet progress seems to be made. From time to time the initial perceptions change. Sometimes these changes in the way an object is percieved lead to a sudden solution. This sudden solution is often accompanied by an experience of insight, known as the "aha!" experience.

1. Evaluate this statement: Some of the greatest advances in science and other fields of knowledge have been made by problem seekers rather than problem solvers. (C,AN,E)

_____
_____
_____
_____

2. The "aha!" experience may accompany the solution of a simple problem as well as a complex one. Have you ever had such an experience? If so, describe how it felt. Explain why an "aha!" experience can also accompany wrong solutions. (C,AP,AN)

_____
_____
_____
_____

Views of the Problem Solving Process

4-Stage View of the Problem Solving Process

This view is based upon the accounts of creative people who have described their own processes of problem solving. It is useful as a general framework. The 4 stages are: (1) preparation, in which the individual becomes acquainted with the problem and plays with some ideas; (2) incubation, during which the individual puts the problem aside and does no conscious work on it (this stage is sometimes skipped); (3) illumination, (also called the "insight" or "aha!" experience) at which time the individual suddenly realizes what he believes to be the solution; and (4) verification, during which the general solution is tested.

A Funneling View of the Problem Solving Process

This approach, developed by German psychologist Karl Duncker, is based upon laboratory observations of what people say and do as they attempt to solve a problem. Duncker saw the process as consisting of three main levels of mental organization. The first level of organization is the general range in which the individual restates the problem and sets forth the general direction or method which might lead to a solution. The second stage, the functional solution, narrows the range; the individual specifies that if such and such could be achieved, the problem would be solved. The third stage is the specific solution. If the specific solution is proved to be correct, the process is over. If not, the individual must go back to stage 2 and if still unsuccessful stage 1.

The Skill View of the Problem Solving Process

A third approach to the problem solving process is to view it as a skill. Like other complex skills, such as driving a car, playing the piano, or playing baseball, thinking involves the coordination and sequencing of many subskills.

Information Processing View of the Problem Solving Process

This approach treats the thinking process as if it were a computer program. Researchers have developed programs to simulate human problem solving.

3. Analyze the implications for education of conceiving productive thinking as a skill. (C,AN)

_____

_____

4. Suppose you wanted to teach a course in Creative Problem Solving. Write a course description for it. Be sure to state the objectives of the course. (C,AP,AN,S)

Creative Problem Solving 101 - _____

_____

_____

_____

_____

_____

Factors That Influence Problem Solving

Many factors influence problem solving. The spatial arrangement of objects and events involved in a problem can help or hinder the finding of a solution. Functional fixity, or the inability to see new uses for familiar objects, also affects problem solving. Sometimes time influences our perception of a problem. For example, if two events occur close together, we might jump to the conclusion that one event caused the other. We might be influenced by the number of objects or facts in the situation; we might be missing facts essential to the solution or there might be so many that we are distracted!

5. Studies have been done to determine the relation between problem solving efficiency and degree of motivation. Speculate as to their results. Draw a graph that represents your view. (C,AP,AN)

6. Although given the same information for A and B, it is easier to solve problem B. Use this example to illustrate how spatial arrangement can influence problem solving. (C,AP)

For each, find the area of the square:

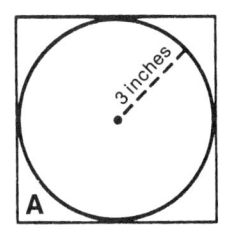

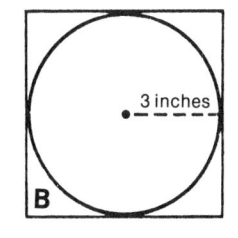

7. Draw a picture that shows someone overcoming "functional fixity" in order to arrive at a solution to a problem. (C,AP,S,E)

8. Analyze the ways in which personal factors, or enduring characteristics of the individual, interact in their effects upon problem-solving proficiency. (C,AN)

_____
_____
_____

19

Intelligence

It is generally agreed that intelligence is made up of a variety of related abilities. Most psychologists would include such things as the abilities to learn, to adapt to new situations, to deal with complex and abstract material, to perceive spatial relationships and to be creative.

Although unable to agree on a definition, most psychologists agree on the usefulness of testing "intelligence." The first standardized tests were developed in the early 1900's. In 1904 the French government asked psychologist Alfred Binet and physician Theophile Simon to develop a test to identify mentally deficient school children so that they could be given special attention. The test they developed was so accurate at predicting the academic performance of students that this type of testing became standard almost immediately. One of the best known versions is the Stanford-Binet test, revised by noted Stanford psychologist L.M. Terman.

1. The Binet-Simon test measures chronological age in relation to mental age. Psychologists express this relationship in the equation:

$$\frac{\text{Mental Age (MA)}}{\text{Chronological Age (CA)}} \times 100 = \text{Intelligence Quotient (IQ)}$$

This ratio is valid until adolescence, when mental growth begins to reach a plateau.

Figure out the IQ of the following children: (K,C)

(A) MA = 8   (B) MA = 5   (C) MA = 8
    CA = 5   CA = 8   CA = 8

(A) IQ = ___   (B) IQ = ___   (C) IQ = ___

2. Some critics of intelligence tests given in schools complain that they are culturally biased. Devise a question that an 8-year-old raised in a specific culture could answer easily, but which would be difficult for a child brought up in a different culture. (C,AP,AN,E,S)

3. Studies indicate that birth order and family size can affect IQ scores. Generally, children in large families have slightly lower average IQ scores. The first born seems to have the advantage, with the first born of a 2-child family doing best. Analyze the reasons for these results. (AN)

_____

_____

_____

_____

Sensation and Perception

Physical energy surrounds us in many forms and in many degrees of intensity. Our senses receive this energy and give us our information about the world around us. Sensations are the simple experiences which result from the physical stimulation of our sensory reception. Perception is the meaningful interpretation of these sensory experiences.

Although people often refer to our five senses, there are actually more. <u>Vision</u>, or sight, is transmitted by the eyes and occipital lobes of the brain. <u>Audition</u>, or hearing, is mediated by the ears and temporal lobes of the brain. <u>Olfaction</u>, or smell, involves the olfactory membranes of the nasal cavity. <u>Gustation</u>, or taste, is mediated by receptor cells in the skin of the tongue, mouth and nose. Our <u>somesthetic senses</u>, such as pressure, pain, warmth and cold, are mediated by the skin. These senses are often referred to as the sense of touch. <u>Kinesthesia</u>, or the sensation of bodily movement, arises from the stimulation of receptors in the muscles, tendons and joints. These kinesthetic sensations help us to keep track of our posture and to guide our movements. <u>Vestibular sensation</u>, or the sense of balance and movement, arises from structures in the inner ear.

1. Occasionally the perception chain is flawed and a misperception occurs. Chart the difficulties which may arise. Illustrate your chart with examples of each. (C,AP)

2. Which do you think is your most valuable sensory organ? Support your choice with facts. (C,AN,E)

_____

_____

_____

3. There are four basic taste qualities: sweet, sour, bitter and salty. Taste is not a very rich sense; in fact, many qualities that we ascribe to taste should be credited to our sense of smell. Blindfold a friend. Ask your friend to taste several common foods while holding his/her nose. See how many foods he can identify. Then have him/her "taste" the same foods without holding his/her nose. Report your findings. (C,AP)

Perceptual Organization

Perception is an organized experience. Even though the organization seems to be spontaneous, it does tend to follow certain general principles.

One of the principles involved in perceptual organization is
<u>assimilation,</u> or the tendency for the difference in intensity be-
tween adjacent parts of a field to be minimized in perception.
Sometimes the differences are not seen at all, even though they are
above the threshold. Opposite of the process of assimilation is
the process of <u>contrast</u>. This occurs when the differences in intensity exceed a certain level. The differences then are perceived as
greater than they are.

Another form of perceptual organization is figure-ground dif-
ferentiation. Parts of a pattern stand out as figure and others
are perceived as ground (background). Size, location and shape
are among the factors that determine which areas will be perceived
as figure. Generally, simple, regular forms tend to be perceived
as figure. Contour, or a line that separates one area of a perceptual field from the adjacent area, is usually perceived as belong-
ing to the figure. There is also a tendency to perceive familiar
and meaningful figures as complete or closed even when they are not.

4. The gray ring appears to be uniformly bright. Place a thin pen
or pencil along the line where the black and white meet. Explain
why the right half of the gray ring now appears darker. (C,AP)

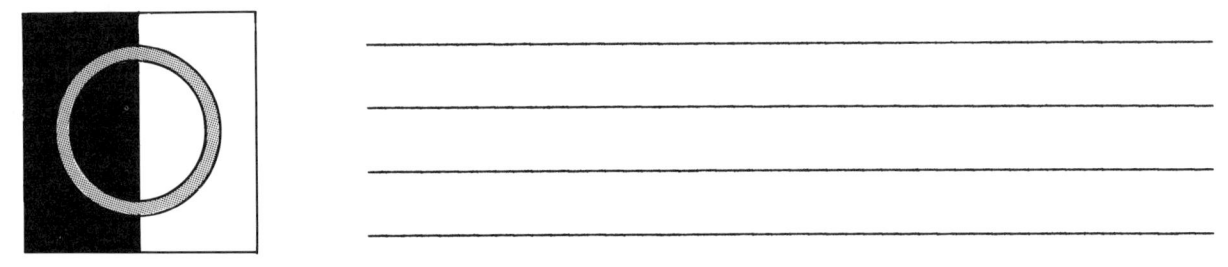

Few of our perceptions involve a single figure-ground pattern.
Many times figures share a common ground. When several figures are
present, we tend to perceptually group them. They may be grouped
according to their proximity, or nearness, to one another; according to their similarity (shape, color, etc.) or according to the
principle of good figure (good continuation, symmetry, closure, etc.).

5. Sometimes the grouping principles work together and help us
define the figure. At other times the grouping tendencies com-
pete with one another. Draw a picture that shows how competition
among grouping principles can be used to one's advantage. (C,AN)

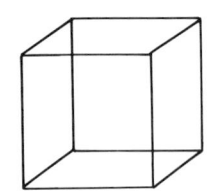

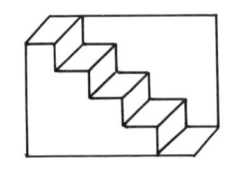

Perceptions may change even if there is no change in the
stimulus pattern. Sometimes we go back and forth between two
alternate organizations. Examples of this type of reversible
figure are the "Necker cube" and the "reversible staircase." In
some cases the perceiver can control the perception by shifting
his visual perception. The Necker cube (left) can be seen as
projecting up or down depending partly upon where you focus your
vision.

6. What do you see? An ugly old woman or a glamorous young lady? Show the picture to several people. Tell some you are showing them an old woman, others that you are showing them a picture of a young one, and show some without telling them anything. Report on your results. (C,AP,AN)

Space and Depth Perception

In experiencing space we receive cues from our senses. The information being received by different senses (or from the same sense) is often incompatible, but one set of cues is often dominant; therefore, we usually get a unified impression of space. While watching a movie, for example, visual cues are dominant. You perceive the sound as coming from the screen even if the speakers are elsewhere.

7. Explain how binaural cues, the stimulus cues occurring at the two ears, make localization of sound easier. How is localization of sound possible when the binaural cues are not sufficient? (C,AP,AN)

_____

_____

Visual stimuli act upon the 2-dimensional retina, but our perception of visual space is a 3-dimensional experience. There are both monocular (pertaining to one eye) cues and binocular (pertaining to both eyes) cues which enable us to perceive depth. Both types must be integrated for a fuller perceptual experience.

8. As far back as 1506 Leonardo da Vinci concluded that our ability to perceive depth and distance is dependent upon factors which we now call monocular depth cues. Make a chart that explains and illustrates monocular depth cues from the visual pattern. Which cue do you think is the most reliable? (C,AP,AN)

9. Relative movement and accomodation are other cues. Accomodation is the readjustment in the lens of the eye to permit the retina to focus on objects at different distances. Relative movement involves the displacement of objects to the left and right as the head moves. Hold a pencil at arm's length so that it is in line with a distant object in the room. Close one eye and move your head horizontally, first to the left and then to the right. Report on your findings. (C,AP,AN)

10. Convergence, or the rotation of the eyes towards each other when looking at an object, and retinal disparity are 2 binocular cues. Explain how retinal disparity is applied in the construction of a stereoscope, an optical instrument that imparts a 3-dimensional effect to a flat picture. (C,AP)

_____

_____

Theoretical Approaches to the Way We Perceive Our World

Although complementary to one another, each of these major approaches differs in emphasis.

The Gestalt Approach - This approach was pioneered by a small group of German psychologists in the early 1900's. "Gestalt" is the German word, loosely translated as "good form" or "good figure." The Gestalt theory states that the brain has innate organizing tendencies and that we tend to see things as "wholes."

The Constructionist Approach - Constructionists believe that we add remembered residuals of previous experiences to present stimulus-induced sensations in order to construct a percept. We select, analyze and add information from our memory banks. In other words, memory provides a familiar context for perceiving.

The Motor Approach - This approach suggests that signals to our muscles become influences on perception and that our developing skills in movement guide our developing motor skills. Critics of this approach admit the importance of eye movements to perception but doubt that other types of movement are as vitally important.

The Ecological Approach - American psychologist J.J. Gibson proposed in 1950 that the normal environment is made up of textured surfaces and that our visual system makes use of the gradients of texture in perceiving our world. He called the perception of textured surfaces "normal" or "ecological" perception. According to this view our perceptual skills get better with age.

The Visual Cliff

Dr. Eleanor Gibson designed an apparatus that gives the illusion of great depth to determine if babies are born with an innate ability to perceive depth. In the middle was a raised wooden plank, painted in a checkerboard pattern. To one side of the plank was a sharp drop off. To the other side, about an inch below the plank, was a normal floor, also with a checkerboard pattern. The entire apparatus was covered with a sturdy glass plate so that the infant was safe from falling. The infants and the animal babies showed an almost immediate awareness of the dangers. They readily explored the floor side but would not go on the cliff side, even when their mothers stood at the side of the apparatus and coaxed them.

11. Later experimenters got slightly different results. A few of the infants and other animal babies did venture over the "cliff." What generalizations can be made based upon these studies? (C,AN)

_____

_____

Conditioning, Learning and Memory

There are many ways in which we learn, remember and forget. Some might consider habituation to be the simplest form of learning. Habituation is the decrease in response to a specific stimulus. It makes it possible to ignore strong, repeated stimuli that would otherwise interfere with other types of learning. When we speak of learning, however, most people consider it to be more than getting used to a new stimulus; they think of learning as being a direct, lasting result of certain experiences.

Classic Conditioning

Conditioning involves the training of an individual to respond in a specific way to a specific stimulus. The scientist who did the most to enhance our understanding of this type of learning was Russian physiologist Ivar Pavlov (1849-1936). He became interested in the phenomenon while experimenting with dogs in his study of digestion.

Pavlov was trying to measure the amount of saliva produced by the dogs. He put them in a harness and then gave them the food. (Animals salivate automatically when given food; they do not have to be taught.) Pavlov noticed, however, that the dogs soon began to salivate before they were given the food - at the mere rattle of the dish or even at the oncoming footsteps of the experimenter. What he learned from this is what we call conditioned-response learning.

The food is called an unconditional or unconditioned stimulus (UCS) because its power to evoke salivation is not conditional upon learning. Salivation, which is innately determined, is called an unconditional response or reflex (UCR). It may be diagrammed in this way:

```
                  innate stimulus-response
    UCS _____connection_____ UCR
   (food)                                (salivation)
```

Suppose you want to train the dog to salivate at a neutral stimulus, such as the sound of a bell. A neutral stimulus is one that does not normally evoke a particular unconditional response. If you pair the neutral stimulus (bell) with the unconditional stimulus (food) enough times, the animal comes to associate the two. This pairing procedure is called reinforcement. When the animal hears the bell, it anticipates that it is about to be fed and, therefore, salivates to the tone of the bell. The bell is called a conditional, or conditioned, stimulus (CS) because its power is conditional upon its being paired with the food. We can diagram the situation like this:

```
         learned stimulus-                  innate stimulus-
   CS    stimulus connection    UCS        response connection    UCR
  (bell)                       (food)                         (salivation)
```

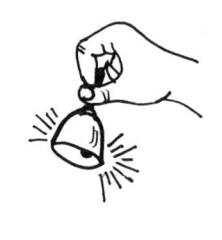

Once the animal has made the connection between the bell and the food, the bell alone can be used to evoke partial salivation. The partial salivation is called the conditional response (CR). Now we can diagram the situation this way:

```
CS            learned stimulus-response            CR
(bell)  _____   (partial
                                                    salivation)
```

There are several factors that affect conditioning. The more often the CS and the UCS are paired, the stronger the CR. The best time to present the CS is immediately before the UCS. Once you establish the CS-CR connection, the animal will sometimes generalize and make the same response if a stimulus is similar to, although not exactly like, the CS. With further training the generalization can be restricted so that the animal discriminates, or responds only to a narrow range of stimuli.

Even after the CS-CR connection is firmly established, the USC and CS must be paired frequently enough for the animal to maintain the association. If not, the CS-CR connection will weaken and eventually be extinguished. An extinguished response, however, is not completely forgotten and is easily relearned. Sometimes, after a period of time, a previously-extinguished response returns with no additional training. This is called spontaneous recovery.

1. If a conditional response to a certain conditional stimulus is strongly established, the conditional stimulus can then be used as an unconditional stimulus. This process is known as higher-order conditioning. Create a step-by-step instruction booklet on how to train a dog to salivate to a light source using higher-order conditioning. (C,AP)

2. John B. Watson and his wife, Rosalie Raynor, experimented with conditioning using humans as their subjects. One of their most famous experiments dealt with the establishment of emotional responses, such as fear, in children. Their subject was a little boy, whom they conditioned to fear a rat. Previously, the boy had not been afraid of the rat and had played with it with no sign of fear. This type of experimentation is now forbidden by the American Psychological Association's Code of Ethics. Judge whether or not this form of experiment is ethical. Explain why you agree or disagree with its prohibition. (C,AN,E)

_____

_____

_____

Instrumental Learning

Instrumental learning, unlike classic conditioning, represents adaptive behavior. It comprises trial-and-error learning and instrumental conditioning, also called operant conditioning. Trial-and-error learning is the process of discovering and then consistently performing the correct response when a number of alternatives exist. Instrumental conditioning is similar to classic conditioning but it differs from it in two important ways. First of all, the final response which is to be learned is not automatically evoked by an unconditional stimulus. The subject must discover the appropriate response. Secondly, in classic conditioning the individual's response does nothing to change or control the situation. In instrumental learning the learned response affects what happens to the individual.

Trial-And-Error Learning

About the same time that Pavlov was doing his work with classic conditioning in Russia, educational psychologist Edward Lee Thorndike (1874-1949) was doing his work in America. His approach was different, however. The principles he formulated came to be known as trial-and-error learning.

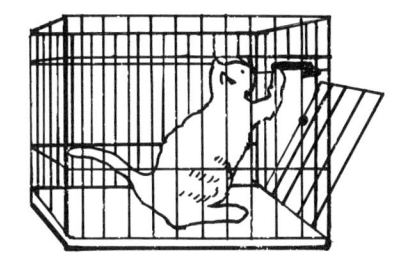

Thorndike believed that humans descend from lower animals and learn in a similar manner. To learn how animals learn, Thorndike studied animals such as chicks, rabbits and cats. His most famous experiments involved an apparatus called a "puzzle box." The animal, such as a cat, was placed inside the box. If the cat figured out how to unlatch the door, it escaped and was rewarded with food. Thorndike noticed that with each experiment the cat at first showed random behavior; it tried many things, such as pacing, squeezing through the bars and clawing and biting at various objects in the box. In time the cat would accidentally bump into the latch and the door would open. The cat escaped and was given the food award. With each subsequent trial the animal eliminated some incorrect responses until it learned - by trial and error - what was required of it and only the successful responses remained.

Thorndike formulated two basic laws of learning based upon his experiments: the law of exercise and the law of effect. The law of exercise asserts that those responses made most frequently and most recently in a given situation are the responses most likely to be made and that the stimulus-response (S-R) connections are strengthened by repetition. The law of effect is based upon the principle of reinforcement. It states that "satisfiers," or rewards, strengthen S-R connections and that punishment weakens S-R connections. At first Thorndike believed that punishment broke S-R bonds; later he revised the law to state that it only suppresses the responses temporarily.

Edward C. Tolman held a different view of trial-and-error learning. Tolman was a Gestalt psychologist. Like other Gestalt psychologists, he believed that animals were capable of higher intellectual activities than those shown by Thorndike's puzzle boxes. Gestalt psychologists believed that animals are capable of "insight." He believed that during these trials the individual is given the opportunity to discover what works and what doesn't in a given situation. He must discover the consequences of <u>all</u> the observed cues not only the correct acts. Unlike Thorndike, Tolman believed that reinforcements (rewards and punishments) are important in adaptive behavior (performance) but not in the learning process.

1. Tolman held the view that one learns by experience but that the learning may not show up in performance until it is useful to the learner; for example, until the situation is changed and a reward is offered for the behavior. Evaluate your own learning experiences in terms of this theory. (C,AN,E)

_____

_____

_____

Instrumental Conditioning

Instrumental conditioning involves following a given response with a reinforcing stimulus. If the response is strengthened as a result of that reinforcement, the individual is said to be conditioned.

The procedure was developed by the American psychologist B.F. Skinner (1904-   ) and is the theoretical approach most widely followed in schools today. Skinner called this type of learning "operant" conditioning, for the individual must learn how to operate on its environment in order to get the desired reinforcement. His most famous experiments involved a pigeon in an apparatus now known as the "Skinner Box." The Skinner Box has a small, round window that can be illuminated. In a typical experiment the pigeon is conditioned to peck at the window when it is lit by rewarding the hungry bird with a pellet of food each time it makes the correct response. At first the pigeon pecks at the window no matter how it is lit. If food is given only when the light is a certain color (or other quality), the bird soon learns to peck at the window only when the light is that color. If the experimenter stops giving the food upon the correct responses, these nonreinforced trials lead to extinction of the conditioning. Like in classic conditioning, however, some aftereffect remains. This aftereffect, or savings, makes it easier to recondition the animal. In other words, fewer reinforcement trials are necessary to reestablish the extinguished response.

There are different types of reinforcement: positive and negative. Reward training uses <u>positive reinforcement</u>; the individual receives something good every time the correct response is made and, therefore, makes that response more often. <u>Negative reinforcement</u> is used in escape training and avoidance training. In this case an unpleasant situation or stimulus is removed when the correct response is made. <u>Punishment</u> involves the application of an unpleasant stimulus in order to weaken a particular response.

Sometimes secondary reinforcement occurs. This phenomenon is similar to higher-order conditioning in classic conditioning. Let's go back to the pigeon in the Skinner Box. Suppose that when the bird pecks at the window, each peck causes the window to be illuminated briefly at the same time that the food pellet is released. Although the light did not begin as a reinforcer, it acquires value as a reward; we call it secondary reinforcement because it gets this reward value from having previously been conditioned to a primary reinforcer.

2. Experiments have shown that partial reinforcement (when the correct response is not always followed by reinforcement) is more resistant to extinction than a habit learned under 100 percent reinforcement. Analyze the factors that contribute to this resistance. (C,AN)

_____
_____
_____
_____

3. Teach an animal to perform an activity using instrumental conditioning. (C,AP,S)

4. Compare and contrast classic and instrumental conditioning. (C,AN)

_____
_____
_____
_____
_____
_____
_____

Memory

Your memory is a storage system for all your past experiences. Without memory you would not be able to recreate or reproduce your past perceptions, emotions, thoughts and actions. There seem to be at least 3 different kinds of memory: sensory memory, short-term memory and long-term memory.

<u>Sensory memory</u> represents the first stage of memory. Your sensory receptors store an exact copy of a stimulus, but hold the input in storage for only a fraction of a second. It is then "erased" by the next input. Afterimages are examples of sensory memory.

<u>Short-term memory</u> is longer than sensory memory, but is still of a short duration. It stores the input for a few seconds (a minute at most) while your brain interprets the meaning of the stimulus. Many psychologists believe that the input is often stored in the form of auditory codes. Short-term memory has a very limited capacity. For example, if an individual is given a list of items, such as a string of digits, to repeat immediately, he will most likely have trouble remembering more than 6 or 7 items. This is because each new item that is added interferes with the preceding ones.

If an item drops out of short-term memory storage, it is usually lost unless your brain decides to enter the input in <u>long-term memory</u>. Any memory that lasts longer than a minute is considered part of this system. Long-term memory seems to involve very complex processes of organizing material for storage, such as clustering. <u>Clustering</u> is the tendency to recall items in meaningful groups. This phenomenon occurs even when the items are presented in a random manner. During the retention period the items are grouped in such a way as to form meaningful clusters. These clusters include such categories as the item's identity, class, attributes, context, function and sensory associations. They may also include the sound and visual pattern of the words used to represent the item.

1. The average person has trouble repeating more than 6 or 7 random digits; however, many can remember a new long distance phone number even though it involves 11 digits. Ask 10 people to immediately recall a series of 11 digits. Ask another 10 people of similar educational background to immediately recall the same 11 digits, but present them as a telephone number. Analyze your results. (C,AP,AN)

2. Some studies have indicated that short-term memory involves acoustic coding of stimuli even when they are presented visually. An experiment performed by R. Conrad in the mid-1960's involved the rapid visual presentations of the letters B-C-F-M-N-P-S-T-V-X in 6-letter sequences. Subjects were required to immediately recall the letters. Most mistakes involved substitution of sound-alikes rather than look-alikes. Do this or a similar experiment with at least 10 subjects and analyze your results. (C,AP,AN)

3. Many psychologists believe that forgetting is due to interference. There are 2 kinds of interference: proactive interference is caused by previously learned material and retroactive interference is caused by subsequently learned material. Use the phenomenon of interference to explain why it is easier to remember the items at the beginning and end of a list. (C,AP)

___

Amnesia

Amnesia is the process by which stored information is erased from your memory bank, blocked from easy access or prevented from being stored. Most amnesia involves the forgetting of language skills rather than motor skills. For example, the patient might not be able to identify an automobile as such but still be able to drive one.

It takes about 20 to 30 minutes for an input or experience to be filed away in long-term memory. A trauma during this so-called <u>consolidation period</u> can prevent the input from being permanently stored. This type of amnesia is called <u>retrograde amnesia</u>. You would probably forget everything that happened immediately after the trauma, most of what happened 5 minutes before and some of what happened 20 minutes before.

4. Anterograde amnesia, which is caused by severe brain damage or certain diseases associated with old age, involves a different type of forgetting. Predict which items would be affected by anterograde amnesia. (C,AN)

Motivation and Emotion

Throughout the years scholars have debated the nature of human motivation. Some took the view that people are mere pawns in the hands of fate; some believed humans to be rational beings who act according to the rational analysis of a situation; some thought of humans as complex machines; some saw humans as products of their environment; some believed unconscious motives are behind most of our behavior; and still others believed motivation to be the result of simple biological drives.

Deficiency Motivation

Deficiency motivation involves the idea that an organism is impelled to action to obtain something important to its survival or to avoid or escape a danger or threat. This physiological approach is sometimes called <u>drive theory</u>. It is based upon the concept of homeostasis, or the tendency of an organism to move toward a need-free or drive-free condition. Drive theorists admit there are other motives besides biological pain and pleasure; however, they refer to these needs as "secondary" needs. They believe an individual learns these needs by associating them with the satisfaction of a primary need.

Some psychologists, such as arousal theorists, criticize the drive theory because they believe there are other important innate needs besides biological ones. They call some of these needs, such as the informational need of most young children to explore their environment, "intra-psychic" needs. They refer to other needs, such as the need of newborn animals to identify with a mother-figure, as social needs.

1. Primary motives are described by drive theorists as those necessary for the preservation of the individual and the species. Make a chart of primary human motives. (C,AP)

Abundancy Motives

Many psychologists agree that some motives, sometimes called abundancy motives, cannot be considered deficiency motives; they do not remove discomfort or danger. In fact, they often seem to increase tension. These abundancy motives include the desires to experience enjoyment, to obtain gratification, to understand and discover, to seek novelty and to achieve. In the mid-1950's Abraham Maslow tried to devise a scheme that would encompass both deficiency and abundancy motives. He concluded that humans move up a hierachy of needs.

MASLOW'S LADDER OF HUMAN MOTIVATION

(1) Biological needs, such as hunger and thirst;

(2) Safety needs, such as security and stability;

(3) Belongingness and love needs, such as affection and identification;

(4) Esteem needs, such as prestige and self-respect; and

(5) The need for self-actualization.

The lower needs must be somewhat satisfied before the individual can pursue the higher-abundancy needs; however, the lower level needs do not have to be completely gratified before the individual moves to the next level.

Another attempt to account for both deficiency and abundancy motives was the arousal theory. This theory is based upon the assumption that homeostasis is a point of optimum arousal rather than a point of zero neural excitation (such as the classical drive theorists believed). Arousal theorists concluded that a decrease in sensory inputs result in boredom and can be as arousing as an increase in biological drives. The optimum point seems to be somewhere between complete stability and complete unpredictability.

2. Make a poster that describes the 5 stages according to Maslow. Illustrate each stage with a picture or drawing of you at each level of development. Explain what is meant by "self-actualization." (C,AP,AN,E)

Emotion

Like the word, "motivate," the word "emotion" also comes from the Latin word "movere," meaning to move or to disturb. Biologically oriented scientists view emotion as a physical reaction which either arouses the body to specific action or depresses physical responses. Some view emotions as different mental experiences, such as fear or anger. Some view them as behavioral responses, such as fearful responses or angry responses. Still others take a bipolar view; they view emotions as being either pleasant or unpleasant. By the 1970's most psychologists came to agree that emotions are too complex to be considered mere hormonal and neural activity. Intra-psychic factors must also be considered. Intra-psychic psychologists attempt to explain actions in terms of an individual's perceptions, motives, values and past experiences.

Although it is difficult to characterize specific emotions and to differentiate between them, there are four general dimensions that can be considered: the <u>intensity</u> of the feeling; the level of <u>tension</u>, or the impulse toward action; the <u>hedonic</u> tone, or the degree of pleasantness or unpleasantness; and the degree of <u>complexity</u>. These general schema can be used to characterize any emotional state.

There are several types of emotional states. <u>Primary emotions</u> (joy, anger, fear and grief) are the most basic. They are usually associated with goal striving and tend to have high degrees of tension. Another class of emotions includes <u>those that pertain to sensory stimulation</u>, such as pain, disgust and delight. Other emotions, such as feelings of success, failure, pride, shame, guilt and remorse, pertain to <u>self-appraisal</u>. Still others pertain to <u>other people and objects</u>; this class includes love and hate. <u>Appreciative emotions</u>, such as humor, beauty and wonder, are characterized by an appreciative orientation towards objects and events.

3. Match each primary emotion with the essential situational condition associated with it. (K,C)

___ Joy   (A) Lack of power to handle threatening situation
___ Anger   (B) Striving toward goal and achieving it
___ Fear   (C) Loss of something sought or valued
___ Grief   (D) Blocking of goal attainment

4. Make an "emotion" booklet. Draw pictures that show situations that cause you to experience various emotions. (C,AP)

The Autonomic Nervous System

The autonomic nervous system controls your emotions. It is sub-divided into the parasympathetic nervous system and sympathetic nervous system. The two systems work together to maintain a balance between over-arousal and under-arousal. The <u>sympathetic nervous system</u> consists of two chains of ganglia (groups of nerve cells) that run along the sides of the spinal cord; there are 22 ganglia in all. From each of these ganglia, axonic fibers run to all the parts of the body. It is the sympathetic nervous system that arouses, or turns on, the emotions.

The <u>parasympathetic nervous system</u> slows down or turns off emotional activity in order to return the body to normal. Although it connects to most parts of the body, it does not connect to all parts. This system is also more specific in its discharge to the various parts of the body than is the sympathetic nervous system, whose discharge is more general.

5. The sympathetic system is connected to the adrenal glands. The adrenal glands secret two hormones, epinephrine and nor-epinephrine (previously known as adrenalin and nor-adrenalin). These are known as the "arousal hormones." Arousal by the sympathetic system is quick, while arousal by the adrenal hormones is needed for sustained arousal. Draw a cartoon depicting a situation in which your epinephrine and nor-epinephrine were flowing. (C,AP,S)

6. In 1884 Harvard professor William James proposed that emotions are responses to bodily reactions that have already occurred and not vice versa. In 1885 Carl G. Lange proposed a similar theory. Evaluate the James-Lange theory of emotions. (C,AN,E)

_____
_____
_____

7. Can we tell a person's emotions by noting facial expressions? Look through photo albums or magazines. Block out the parts of the pictures that show the situation. Have others try to guess the people's emotions. Write a generalization based upon your results. (C,AP,AN)

Altered States of Consciousness

Consciousness may be generally defined as the process of being aware of one's bodily condition and one's surroundings. We refer to this state of mental functioning as a normal state of consciousness (NSC). All of us, however, experience states of consciousness which are different from our normal states. These so-called altered states of consciousness (ASC) include common experiences such as the hypnagogic state (on the verge of falling asleep) sleeping and dreaming. They also include hypnotic states, peak experiences, meditative states and alcohol- and other drug-induced states.

1. The hypnagogic state lasts only a few minutes and is usually forgotten as soon as the individual reaches the next phase of sleep; however, many creative people claim that this stage is a rich source of ideas. Try this technique to make yourself aware of your thoughts during this state. Lie down with your elbow resting on the bed. Raise your lower arm to a vertical position, keeping the hand and arm straight up. When you pass the hypnagogic state and are about to go into dreamless sleep, your arm will probably fall and wake you. Write down the thoughts that are in your mind at the time. (C,AP)

Dreaming

Dreaming is the most common ASC in western culture. The elements of our dreams are usually taken from our every-day world, but we tend to reorganize them in unusual fashions. The main difference between our dream state and our NSC is our willingness to accept strange happenings.

2. Write a humorous story in which a dream turns into reality. (S)

3. There are several stages of sleep; they go from light sleep (stage 1) to deep sleep (stage 4). Usually, we go to REM sleep after stage 4. REM is an acronym. For what words do the letters stand? (K)

R_____ E_____ M_____

4. Most dreaming seems to occur during REM sleep. Roger Sperry, a pioneer in split-brain surgery, reported that many of his patients reported having vivid dreams before surgery; however, none of these patients reported having dreams after split-brain surgery. Although the evidence is not conclusive, what do Sperry's findings tend to indicate? (C,AN)

_____

_____

Nightmares

There are two kinds of nightmares. Anxiety nightmares are quite common. Like most dream experiences, they occur during REM sleep. There are few bodily changes and the content of the dream itself seems to lead to the anxiety attack. Classic examples are the feelings that you are being chased or that you are falling.

A much more disturbing experience is an incubus nightmare, or night terror. The night terror begins in the deep sleep of stage 4. The pulse becomes extremely slow and breathing almost stops. This seems to cause one of the lower centers in the brain to panic and respond as if the individual were being suffocated. A classic example is the feeling that a cat-like beast is on your chest, sucking the life out of your lungs. The victim screams, thrashes about and often runs about trying to rid himself of the creature. Upon awakening, the person knows something awful has happened, but doesn't recall any details!

5. A common anxiety nightmare is trying to run through a thick molasses-like substance but being unable to get very far. Find out what happens to your voluntary muscles during REM sleep that might account for this particular nightmare. (C,AP)

Hypnosis

Hypnosis is an ASC characterized by increased susceptibility to suggestion. In general, it seems that children are easier to hypnotize than adults. Hypnotic phenomena include hyperesthesia, or an increased sensitivity; hypoesthesia, or a decreased sensitivity; hallucinations; and a dissociation of action from awareness. Although hypnosis can be a valuable tool when used properly by a trained therapist, it can be extremely dangerous when practiced by an untrained person!

6. Create a brochure for a worthwhile theraputic use of hypnosis. (C,AP,E)

Alcohol- and Other Drug-Induced States

Drugs can affect our bodies in many ways. One of the most common effects is upon the rapidity of neural firing. Caffeine is an example of a drug that increases the rate at which your neurons fire; it speeds up the release of neuro-transmitters at the excitatory synapses. Barbiturates have an opposite effect. They slow down or inhibit neural activity. Sometimes they slow it down so much that the person falls asleep.

7. Alcohol is one of the most abused drugs. It affects the brain in many ways. One of the most important effects is the selective killing of nerve cells. Think about the behavioral changes associated with chronic drunkenness. Speculate as to the hemisphere where most of the cell damage occurs. (C,AN)

Frustration and Conflict

In any society an individual's wants and needs often conflict with those of the larger group. The restraints and prohibitions imposed upon an individual by the society are often a source of conflict and frustration. As the individual internalizes the standards of the society (in other words, as they become a part of himself), the conflict turns inward.

Although more attention is paid to the disruptive nature of frustration and conflict, there are also constructive effects. They may serve to focus the person's attention on the particular motive. The increased motivation may cause the individual to disregard other motives, needs and desires and to perceive the unattained goal as even more desirable. These factors in turn lead to <u>intensified striving</u> to reach the goal.

Sometimes the intensified striving is all that is needed to attain the goal. At other times, however, the barrier blocking attainment is too strong. If the effect of the frustration is to remain constructive, the individual must once again evaluate the situation. Perhaps he must find a <u>new course of action</u> in order to achieve the goal. Maybe he must find a <u>new goal</u> altogether; however, if the substitute goal is not as desirable and the individual must make some sort of compromise, he might still feel some tension.

When intensified striving, trying new courses of action and substituting other goals fail to solve the problem, the individual must make more fundamental changes. The situation itself must be redefined. Choices between alternatives must be made. New elements might have to be added. For example, a young person's conflicting desires to be aggressive and to be liked might lead to the decision to run for class president.

If none of the constructive effects of frustration and conflict are successful in bringing about achievement of the goal, the tension continues to mount. Eventually, it leads to disruption. The striving might build to such a point that it is no longer appropriate for that goal. Perhaps the individual has focused on the unattainable goal to such an extent that he fails to see viable alternatives. In many cases the emotional agitation causes the individual to lose control and panic.

Disruptive Effects of Frustration

At this point disruptive effects of the frustration appear. Two of the most common effects are aggression and escape. <u>Aggression</u> in the form of a direct attack upon the obstacle may be considered adaptive behavior. Often, however, the aggression fails to solve the problem. In many cases there is no identifiable obstacle to combat; therefore, the individual generalizes his anger. He may lash out at anything. When an individual shifts a feeling towards a substitute object, it is called <u>displacement</u>.

The other common effect, escape, may offer temporary relief; however, it does nothing to help attain the goal. The original motive remains and the tension increases. Chronic escape reactions and frustration may lead to personality disorders, such as regression, or the manifestation of less mature behavior than previously shown.

1. Evaluate this statement: "We often perceive goals as more desirable when they appear unattainable. It is at that point that motive strength is greatest." (C,AN,E)

_____

_____

_____

2. Frustration tolerance is the threshold for the maximum amount of frustration an individual can withstand before disruptive patterns of behavior develop. Individuals vary in their levels of tolerance. The same individual may even show different levels of tolerance at different times. Describe a frustrating situation towards which you or someone you know showed a different level of tolerance at different points in time. Analyze the reasons for the different reactions. (C,AN,E)

_____

_____

_____

_____

3. In some situations the frustrated individual cannot express his anger directly at the source and, therefore, takes out the anger on someone else. This is called displacement. Create a comic strip that illustrates this type of defense mechanism. (C,AP,S)

Short-Term Conflicts

Most people have more than one motive at a time. Often our motives conflict with one another. The short-term conflicts most of us face have only temporary effects.

4. Goals may conflict in several ways. Cite examples of the following patterns of conflict. Explain which are likely to cause the most and least anxiety. (C,AP,AN)

    A. A person must choose between two positive goals.

    B. The same goal has both positive and negative aspects.

    C. The person must choose between two negative goals.

Mental Disorders

When an individual is unable to realistically cope with everyday life, we say the person has a mental disorder. Sometimes the condition occurs because the person's defense mechanisms have not protected him from the anxiety of psychological conflicts. In other cases the defense mechanisms may have worked too well! If a defense mechanism comes to dominate a person's behavior, the person loses his sense of reality.

The DSM

In 1952 the American Psychiatric Association published the first edition of the Diagnostic and Statistical Manual of Mental Disorders (DSM-I). The third edition (DSM-III) was published in 1980. It was an attempt to give specific analysis for every patient who might be referred to a psychologist or psychiatrist. The therapist rates the patient according to each of five axes, or categories:

- AXIS 1 = SEVERE MENTAL DISORDERS, INCLUDING PSYCHOSES AND NEUROTIC DISORDERS
- AXIS 2 = PERSONALITY DISORDERS
- AXIS 3 = PHYSICAL DISORDERS
- AXIS 4 = SOCIAL STRESS SCALE
- AXIS 5 = SCALE TO DESCRIBE HIGHEST LEVEL OF ADAPTIVE FUNCTIONING DURING LAST YEAR

DSM-III marked a change in perspective from DSM-II, published in 1968. DSM-II was somewhat based upon Sigmund Freud's psychoanalytic theory. Freud proposed that most mental illness is due to biological or psychological causes. The severe forms were called psychoses; those that appeared to have biological causes were called organic psychoses and the others were called functional psychoses. Less severe disorders were called neuroses. DSM-III moves away from Freudian psychology. Rather than use the terms "psychosis" and "neurosis," it uses the general term "disorder." The authors of DSM-III take the view that mental disorders are caused by underlying psychological "diseases"; they view psychological problems as medical ones.

1. List several disorders that usually manifest themselves in childhood or adolescence. (K,C)

2. Schizophrenia is a functional psychosis. The term comes from Latin words meaning "splitting of the mind." Research the symptoms and analyze why the term may be misleading. (C,AN)

3. Paranoia is also a functional psychotic disorder. Create a satirical cartoon that illustrates the symptoms. (C,AP)

4. Neuroses (psychoneuroses) are milder forms of mental disorders than psychoses. A phobic neurosis (phobic disorder in the DSM-III) is one in which the individual has an irrational, intense fear of certain objects, places or situations. Make up a phobia matching game. Try to include some unusual ones! (C,AP)

5. Invent 5 humorous phobias and name them appropriately. (C,AP,S)

Psychotic Depression and Manic States

Everyone feels mildly depressed once in a while. It may be a spontaneous feeling or it may be a reaction to an external event. This type of depression usually disappears in time without medical help. True psychotic depression is a more serious matter. The psychotic depressive has a deep, unjustified sadness. He seems to have "given up" and withdraws from everyday activities. Physiological changes also occur, such as insomnia and a loss of appetite. Two kinds of antidepressive drugs are useful in combatting depression: MAO (Monoamine oxidose) inhibitors and tricyclic drugs.

Sometimes people who suffer from depression also have mood swings at the other extreme. These periods of elation, called manic attacks, are characterized by heightened bodily activity and uncontrolled talkativeness. Although these feelings of elation are not likely to be as upsetting to the individual as are the feelings of depression, there is the danger that the patient might harm himself or others while in this state. Drugs containing lithium have been useful in controlling mania.

6. The use of chemotherapy to treat psychotic depression is a form of defense coping. Compare and contrast defense coping and direct coping. (C,AN)

Psychotherapy

There are several theories of personality development and of the techniques and aims of therapy. Each of the major categories of psychotherapy holds a different view of the nature and origin of deviant, or abnormal, behavior.

Psychoanalytic Therapy

Psychoanalytic therapies are based upon Sigmund Freud's theory of personality development. An important principle is that adult behavior is dependent upon the person's early childhood experiences. Neurotic illness is believed to be caused by inner conflicts. The goal of therapy is to bring these conflicts into the individual's conscious awareness and under its control. Dream analysis is an important aspect of psychoanalysis as is free association, the method in which the patient is encouraged to express whatever comes into mind! Sometimes the therapist notices that the patient is resisting certain feelings and memories. The therapist interprets the resistance and helps the patient "reexperience" that which had been blocked from awareness. The reexperiencing, it is believed, will help the patient understand his problems. The therapist must then help the patient use the newly gained insight to make behavioral changes - not always an easy task!

1. <u>Transference</u> is an important phenomenon of psychoanalysis. Define the term and analyze its importance. (C,AN)

2. Write a script for a movie scene in which the main character is being psychoanalyzed and is on the verge of transference. (C,AN,S,E)

3. In classic psychoanalysis the therapist stays behind the patient, out of view. The patient lies on the couch and is encouraged to talk freely. Many modern psychologists practice a modified version, called psychoanalytically oriented psychotherapy. The patient is interviewed face to face rather than lying on a couch. Also, instead of having an emphasis on free association, interviews focus upon the areas of concern. What benefits, if any, does this version have over classic psychoanalysis? (C,AN)

Behavior Therapy

Behavior therapies are based upon the principles of conditioning and instrumental learning. Neurotic disorders are viewed as learned responses that have evolved into conditioned reflexes. Prime examples are phobias and anxiety. Therapy involves: (1) counterconditioning, or the replacement of responses which are symptomatic of the disorders with new learned patterns, such as relaxation, or (2) conditioning of negative responses to the established patterns of deviant behavior. Although many behaviorists admit that inner states and processes exist, most feel they should remain outside their area of concern, for they are not directly observable.

4. Use the principles of conditioning to explain the behaviorist view of how a phobia is acquired. (C,AP)

_____
_____
_____

Desensitization Therapy

Desensitization therapy is a behavior modification technique developed by Joseph Wolpe. It involves three basic steps. Step 1 is training the patient to relax. Step 2 involves the establishment of a hierarchy of fears. The patient lists all of the stimuli that disturb him in the order of their severity - from lowest to highest. The last step involves the gradual pairing of each anxiety-producing stimulus, beginning with the lowest one in the hierarchy, with the relaxed state learned in step 1.

5. Pretend that you are a behavior therapist. Your patient has a phobia about cats. You have already trained him to achieve a relaxed state. After carefully interviewing him, you have established his hierarchy of fears. Explain how you will use the hierarchy to desensitize his fear of cats. (C,AN,AP)

Humanistic Therapy

Humanistic therapy is based upon the principle of self-actualization, the belief that every human has an innate tendency to strive to reach his full potential. The patient rather than the therapist sets the goals. Emphasis is placed upon conscious drives. The present and future are more important than past experiences.

The major goal of therapy is to help the individual reach self-actualization. The patient is encouraged to express hidden thoughts and feelings. It is hoped the individual will gain a clearer perception of himself and a better idea of how others perceive him. The therapist's role is to provide feedback as to his progress. When the individual is able to accept his "real self," psychological integration will have been achieved.

Client-Centered Therapy

Client-centered therapy, sometimes called non-directive therapy, was developed by Carl Rogers in the 1940's. Like most humanistic psychologists, Rogers believed it was inappropriate for a therapist to impose his own values upon his patients, or clients. Rather than give advice, the therapist tries to clarify the nature of the problems. One technique used in this type of therapy is called "reflection of feeling." The therapist restates what the client says in a slightly different way. The therapist tries to build feelings of confidence and trust by accepting whatever the individual says or does without criticism. Rogers said that this "unconditional positive regard" was necessary in order for the client to have enough courage to see himself as he really is.

6. Evaluate Carl Rogers' technique of "Unconditional Positive Regard." Do you think it is possible for a therapist never to impose his own values? How might the therapist unconsciously reinforce those values upon the patient? (AN,E)

_____

_____

_____

Gestalt Therapy

Gestalt therapy is based upon the principles of Gestalt psychology. In the early part of the twentieth century a group of German psychologists, including Max Wertheimer, Kurt Koffka and Wolfgang Köhler, initiated a study of the organized nature of perception. They came to the general conclusion that our brains tend to force all percepts into better or natural shapes. We tend to see things in wholes. Gestalt therapy was developed by Fritz Perls in 1951 and gained in importance during the late 1950's and 1960's. Its name stems from the attempt to help the patient become a "whole" person. The emphasis of Gestalt therapy is on the here and now. Like client-centered therapy, the ultimate goal is for the patient to see himself as he really is by removing the resistances to this awareness. Unlike client-centered and many other humanistic therapists, however, Gestalt therapists think that dreams and fantasies are important as spontaneous forms of expression.

In keeping with the Gestalt principles, pathology is seen as the disowning of parts of oneself and one's experiences. The therapy focuses upon those aspects of the physical, symbolic and interpersonal behavior which represent attempts to resist or block total self-awareness and acceptance. Certain behaviors are clues to avoidance attempts. The therapist points out these clues (folded arms, tapping of fingers, etc.) but never interprets them. It is up to the patient to discover their meanings. In this way the patient cannot deny the interpretation.

Gestalt therapists believe that patients must experience what they have been trying to avoid. They use specific techniques to encourage patients to experiment with new ways of acting and of perceiving themselves and the world around them. Three of these techniques are: playing out a projection, personality reversal and exaggeration of slight unconscious movements.

7. Gestalt therapists feel the patient must take responsibility for himself. Although they do a lot to direct the course of action, most try not to manipulate the patient or the outcome. Many psychoanalysts feel that all therapists have the responsibility to manage the course of therapy. Take a point of view and prepare your closing remarks for a debate. (AN,E)

8. "Playing a projection" is a game technique used in Gestalt therapy. For example, if the patient says the therapist is selfish, the therapist has the patient play the part of a selfish person to become aware of parts of himself that are selfish. Role play the type of person that annoys you most: selfish, unsympathetic, untrustworthy, etc. (C,AP,AN,E)

9. Reversal involves acting in a way opposite to your normal behavior. Draw a picture that illustrates how a therapist would ask you to behave in a reversal game. (C,AP,AN,E)

Interpersonal (Social) Therapy

The focus of interpersonal therapy is upon interpersonal relations. Pathology is viewed as a result of problems in relations and communications among people. Therapy, therefore, attempts to improve interpersonal interaction. Harry Stack Sullivan (1892-1949) was one of the first interpersonal therapists. The emphasis of his therapy was upon the role of the patient-therapist relationship. He believed that the role of the therapist should be that of "participant observer." As such, the therapist must help the patient become aware of his "parataxic distortions." By "parataxic distortions" Sullivan meant those attitudes which are based upon the distorted evaluation of an individual or upon identification of that individual with another from the past.

10. Psychodrama is a technique in which patients (alone or in groups) enact roles in plays which center around problems similar to their own. Analyze the possible benefits of psychodrama. (AN)

_____

_____

_____

Psychosurgery

Psychosurgery is surgery that destroys or removes healthy brain tissue in order to change a patient's behavior.

11. Write a letter to the editor of a scientific journal expressing your view of the use of psychosurgery on patients who are prone to violent behavior. (AN,E)

Personality

Psychologists study personality in an attempt to identify and describe human characteristics. Personality may be broadly defined as an individual's distinctive way of thinking, feeling and behaving. It is the way in which the individual adjusts to the various situations he encounters. Although hereditary factors are important, personality is a constantly-adapting phenomenon.

There are two basic ways in which psychologists describe an individual's personality: in terms of traits and in terms of types. Traits are enduring characteristics that are consistently observed in the individual's behavior. There are different levels of traits. For example, some traits, often called surface traits, are highly observable traits; other traits are deep-seated and not as easily observed. Typologies, or systems for establishing personality types, represent attempts to categorize individuals. Of course, there are few, if any, pure types; therefore, a person is described by the degree to which he resembles the traits representative of the type. Typologies have been criticized because they are artificially established. Even so, certain trait profiles do seem to occur more often than others and, therefore, function as convenient reference points in classifying individuals.

1. Ancient Greek physicians offered a theory of human types which focussed upon emotional attributes of personality. It was based on a rather primitive understanding of physiology. Create a poster explaining the classical Greek theory and illustrating the effects of the imbalance of the humours. (K,C,AP)

2. In the mid-1930's German psychologist Ernst Kretschmer (1888-1964) developed a theory of personality based upon body types. Draw a picture representative of each type. (C,AP)

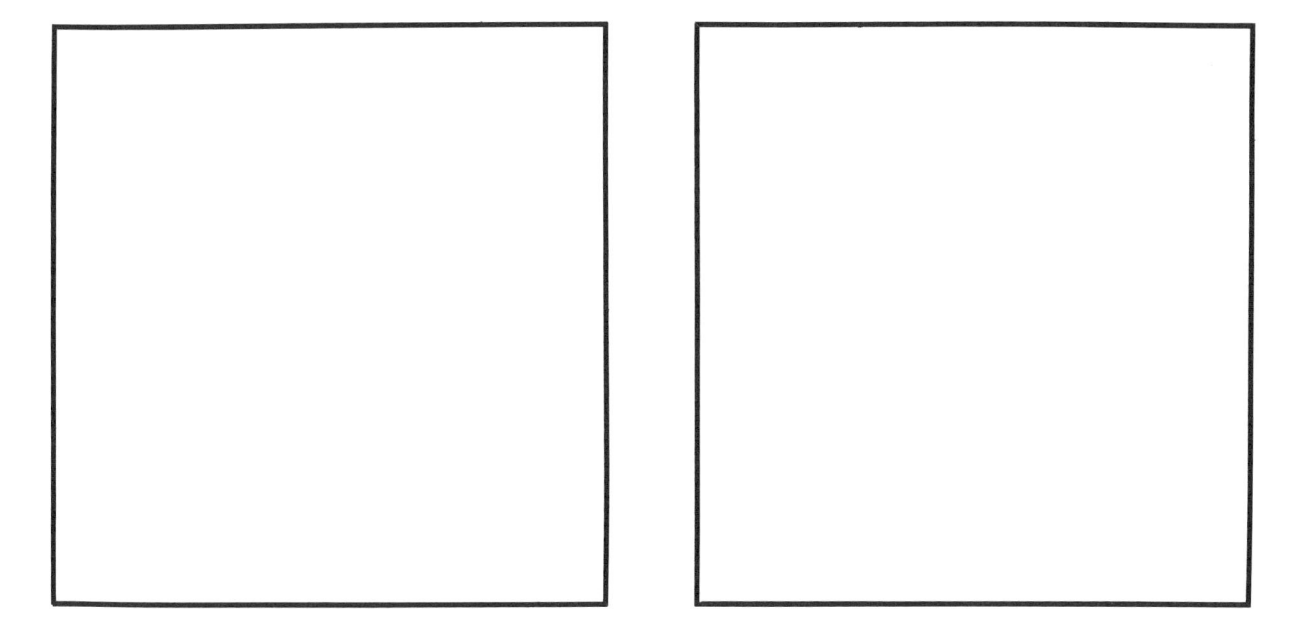

3. Compile a list of adjectives that you would use to describe your personality. (AP,AN,E)

45

4. Francis Galton (1822-1911) was interested in trait theory as it applied to eugenics. He wanted the "gifted" to have more children and those not as intellectually fit to have fewer offspring. Analyze and evaluate Galton's view in both practical and ethical terms. (C,AN,E)

Personality Assessment

Psychologists try to measure personality in terms of degree and number: how much of a trait manifests itself and how many traits are manifested. There are several methods of assessment. Some involve the observation of an individual in realistic social situations. Others are based upon performance in test situations.

Ratings

Ratings are one of the most commonly used forms of personality measurement. The most usual method is normative rating. Normative rating involves the placement of an individual along a rating scale as compared with other individuals in the sample. An adjective checklist is really a two-point rating scale (yes or no). Most, however, attempt to achieve a finer discrimination.

A different approach from normative rating is ipsative rating. Q-sorts are examples of this approach. Rather than rate the individual on a given trait relative to other people, the traits are rated according to their applicability within the individual.

There are several possible sources of data for ratings. The data may be based upon direct observation of the individual's behavior in a variety of settings. The ratings may be based upon information obtained during a personal interview or from a self-rating. Data may also be obtained from documents, work records, test scores, etc.

5. Create and duplicate a list of at least 100 adjectives. Have several individuals (including yourself) check those adjectives they regard as self-descriptive. For each ask a close friend or relative to check off on another copy those adjectives that describe the individual. Compare the results and summarize your findings. (C,AP,AN)

6. Draw 2 pictures. The first as you see yourself. The second as your friend sees you. (C,AP,AN)

Situational Tests

Situational tests involve the observation of individuals in situations devised to replicate real-life. The more realistic the situation, the more valid the test! They may involve the observation of subjects individually or as they interact.

7. Devise a situational test that could be used to measure an individual's honesty. (C,AP,S,E)

Personality Inventories

In a personality inventory an individual is asked to answer questions designed to reflect the person's interests, attitudes, values, emotional adjustment and social relations. One widely used example is the MMPI, or Minnesota Multiphasic Personality Inventory. It is more reliable than many other tests because the scales are standardized by pretesting the items on groups known to be high and low on the trait in question. The subject is asked to answer true, false, or cannot say to each of 550 simple statements. By looking at the profile (pattern) of the scores, the interpreter attempts to determine the areas in which the subject is "normal" and those in which he is "abnormal." Many psychologists believe this test to be valid because it correlates highly with the diagnoses made by trained psychiatrists.

8. Explain the difference between reliability and validity. Analyze why a test can have high reliability and low validity but cannot have low reliability and high validity. (C,AN)

_____

_____

_____

9. Think of 10 questions to include on a personality inventory to measure an individual's aggressive tendencies. (C,AP,AN,E,S)

Projective Techniques

Psychologists use projective techniques to measure deeper aspects of personality. They are based upon the theory that people tend to project their own personalities upon weakly structured or ambiguous stimuli. Two classic examples are inkblot tests and the TAT. Inkblot tests were developed in 1911 by Swiss psychiatrist Hermann Rorschach. In its classic form it is a series of 10 inkblots shown one at a time. The subject is asked to report on what he sees. The TAT is an acronym for Thematic Apperception Test. It was developed in 1935 by Henry Murray. There are 20 pictures, each depicting a vague but potentially emotional situation. For each picture the subject makes up a story to explain the situation, the events that led to the situation and what will happen to the people in the picture. The psychologist uses the themes as clues to the subject's perception of the world.

10. Projective tests have been criticized as being unreliable and not very valid because they depend upon the interpreter's subjective evaluation. Evaluate this statement: "The interpretations from Rorschach tests and TAT's sometimes reveal more about the interpreter than the subject!" (C,AN,E)

_____

_____

_____

Theories of Personality

Personality theorists attempt to develop comprehensive theories to account for all human behavior - a mind-boggling task! There are four main groups of personality theories: (1) <u>trait or type theory</u>, such as that of Francis Galton; (2) <u>psychoanalytic</u> theories, such as those of Sigmund Freud; (3) <u>social-learning</u> theories; and (4) <u>humanistic</u> theories.

Trait Or Type Theory

Every theory of personality involves some notion of traits, or types. There are two main points of emphasis. On the one hand, people share their characteristics with others. On the other hand, every person is unique because of the combination and degree of the characteristics.

Psychodynamic Theories

Psychodynamic theories are based upon the assumption that personality is a result of conflicts among needs or impulses, both conscious or unconscious. The nature of the conflicts and the individual's ways of resolving them form the individual's personality.

Psychoanalysis: Sigmund Freud

Among the most influential of any theories of personality have been Sigmund Freud's theories of psychoanalysis. Freud was born in what is now Czechoslovakia in 1856 but was raised in Vienna. He eventually became a physician and specialized in treating the mentally ill. In 1882 Freud worked with Josef Breuer, a Viennese physician-physiologist who had achieved success using hypnosis with a patient suffering from hysteria. With Breuer, Freud developed a technique called catharsis. "Catharsis" comes from a Greek word meaning "to clear out." They believed that the re-enacting of emotional situations under hypnosis could act as a catharsis by allowing bottled up forces to be released.

Freud gradually abandoned the process of hypnosis. During the years 1892-1895 he developed the technique of free association. Free association is the technique of encouraging patients to recall all aspects of their past and present experiences, including thoughts, feelings or memories without fear of criticism. Freud found that this free association could bring about catharsis without the use of hypnosis. An important goal of free association is to help the patient view traumatic experiences in non-emotional ways. Through free association and dream analysis the analyst helps the patient discover and interpret his experiences and to gain insight into those aspects of the experiences which have been bothering him. Freud called this technique "psychoanalysis."

According to Freud's views, the human personality comprises three principal systems: the id, the ego and the superego. The id is the primitive system and is the source of psychic energy, known as "libido." This psychic energy is in the form of unconscious instinctual drives. The id is driven by the "pleasure principle"; in other words, the id strives to achieve pleasure and avoid pain.

The ego is one's conscious self. It is the ego that remains in contact with reality and serves as the mediator between the id, the superego and the external world. The ego helps the id achieve the satisfaction it seeks.

The superego is the portion of an individual's personality that splits from the ego. It represents the person's internalization of the moral standards of society. There are 2 aspects of superego: "conscience," which is usually acquired from one's parents and "self-ideal," usually acquired from others. This internalization of social norms, or socialization, occurs on the unconscious level.

The arousal of anxiety is seen as the result of conflicts between the id, the ego and the superego. The ego uses defense mechanisms to defend itself against these conflicts with the id and superego. The defense mechanisms reduce the ego's anxiety by denying or distorting reality. They operate on the unconscious levels of our minds. The main defense mechanisms are displacement, regression, repression, reaction formation, rationalization, sublimation and projection.

Freud believed that children pass through a sequence of psychosexual stages. He stressed the importance of early childhood experiences upon the development of an individual. Psychological maturity is dependent upon the successful passage through each period.

Although many of Sigmund Freud's theories have been questioned, his impact upon personality theory has been tremendous!

1. Research the life of Sigmund Freud. Write the script for a TV episode, "This Is Your Life...Sigmund Freud." (C,AP,S)

2. Create a comic strip that describes a conflict among the ego, id and superego. (C,AP,S)

Defense Mechanisms

When conflict and frustration persist, the anxiety causes the individual to exhibit various defense mechanisms in an attempt to cope with his environment and to enhance his self-image. They are effective only if they fool the individual. Everyone uses these defense mechanisms occassionally. It is only when they occur excessively and prevent the individual from facing problems realistically that they become serious problems.

Defense Mechanisms:

Displacement - The shifting of a feeling towards a substitute object.

Regression - The manifestation of a less mature behavior than previously shown.

Repression - The inability to recall anxiety-arousing experiences.

Reaction formation - The exaggerated expression of behavioral tendencies which are opposite of underlying repressed impulses.

Rationalization - The individual finds false reasons to justify illogical, immature or otherwise questionable behavior or situations.

Sublimation - The giving up of an instinctual gratification for a noninstinctual one in order to conform with social values.

Projection - The individual displaces his own unacceptable impulses and traits onto someone else.

3. Which of the described defense mechanisms is the most mature? (C,E)

_____

_____

4. Describe a situation in which someone you know exhibited one of these defense mechanisms. (C,AP)

_____

_____

_____

Carl Jung

Swiss psychologist Carl Jung (1875-1961) was at one time a disciple of Sigmund Freud. Eventually, however, he broke away from Freud and developed his own psychoanalytic theory, which he called "analytic psychology." He believed that our basic motivation stems from moral and spiritual values rather than from primitive sexuality as Freud believed.

Jung called the total personality the "psyche." The psyche is composed of several subsystems, the most important of which are the ego, the personal unconscious and the collective unconscious. The ego, like in Freudian theory, is the conscious aspect of the human mind. It comprises the perceptions, thoughts, memories and feelings available to the individual. The ego is important in helping the person function in everyday life.

Like Freud, Jung believed that unconscious forces are aspects of personality. Jung, however, divided the unconscious mind into two distinct processes: the personal unconscious and the collective unconscious. The personal unconscious comprises experiences and thoughts which the individual has had but which have been blocked from awareness. These individual experiences and thoughts can become conscious once again under the proper circumstances. The collective unconscious refers to the accumulated experiences of the species throughout its evolutionary development which are never directly available to the conscious mind.

Jung called the universal thoughts that he believed to make up the collective unconscious "archetypes." He theorized that these archetypes, or primordial images, were genetically passed on from generation to generation. Most of our information about archetypes is derived from art, dreams, visions, hallucinations and, especially, mythology. Jung did not mean that the definite mythological images and motifs themselves are the archetypes; those he saw as conscious representations. What Jung referred to as archetypes were the tendencies to form such representations of a motif. Although details vary, the basic patterns remain the same.

One of the most widely accepted aspects of Jungian theory has been Jung's ideas on extroversion and introversion. Jung postulated that we are all born with two innate attitudes: extroversion, which leads us toward the external, objective world, and introversion, which leads us to look toward the inner, subjective world. He believed that one of these two attitudes usually predominates in consciousness. The other attitude, however, often expresses itself unconsciously through dreams and fantasies.

According to Jung human beings have an innate drive toward selfhood and wholeness. Selfhood involves the achievement of balance among what he believed to be the four basic functions of the mind: <u>thinking</u> (the intellectual understanding of self and world); <u>feeling</u> (the evaluation of other people, situations and objects in terms of pleasure, pain, etc.), <u>sensing</u> (the perception of reality); and <u>intuition</u> (the unconscious perception of reality). Jung differed from Freud in that he did not place as much emphasis on the early stages of life. Although he agreed that early experiences may hamper a person's development, he thought the focus should be upon what the individual is attempting to achieve rather than the past.

5. One example of Jung's archetypes is his belief in elements he called "anima" and "animus." These terms refer to the elements of the opposite sex that are in every one of us. For males the feminine archetype is anima and for females it is animus. According to Jung these elements developed as a result of the species' experiences with opposite sex members. He believed that a fully integrated adult uses this opposite-sex component to achieve fulfillment. Do you agree or disagree with this theory? (AN,E)

6. Jung noticed that some myths seem to be repeated in many cultures in some variety. Draw a picture that illustrates a recurrent mythological theme. (C,AP)

Social Determinants of Personality: Alfred Adler

Although Alfred Adler (1870-1937) was interested in and influenced by Sigmund Freud, his ideas differed in many important ways from those of Freud. He formed his own group, called the Society for Individual Psychology. Adler and his followers believed that the social environment was of prime importance in determining personality. Our main source of motivation is our innate struggle to achieve superiority or self-realization.

Unlike Freud and Jung who stressed unconscious influences upon human behavior, Adler was convinced that we are usually aware of our motives. He said that we know what our inferiorities are and that we strive to overcome them. Adler called the driving force for completion and perfection the "creative force."

Childhood was important to Adler but not for the same reasons it was important to Freud. Children have intrinsic weaknesses. They learn that there are things that adults can do that they cannot. This creates in us at a young age feelings of <u>inferiority</u>. The feelings of inferiority not only increase our motivation to succeed but also create a drive for compensation. <u>Compensation</u> is the urge to make up for the inferiority by trying to become superior in other ways. The feelings of inferiority themselves are necessary to psychological development. When accompanied by great stress or when compensation continually fails, however, an inferiority complex might develop and hinder adjustment.

The goal of Alderian analysis is to help the individual become aware of the real or imagined weaknesses for which he is attempting to compensate. The individual can then reevaluate his goals as to their practicality.

7. Compensation may be regarded as a defense mechanism. Think about your own behavior. In what ways do you compensate for (real or imagined) defects or weaknesses. (C,AN)

_____

_____

_____

Psychosocial Theory of Development: Erik H. Erikson

Erik H. Erikson was also greatly influenced by Sigmund Freud but he expanded and elaborated upon his theory. Like Freud, he concluded that a child's instinctual drives are important; however, he believed that it is the conflict between those instincts and the cultural demands that determines the child's personality. Also, he believed that development continues into adulthood. Erikson proposed that there are eight developmental stages, each with its characteristic psychosocial crisis.

8. Research and create a chart that shows the characteristic crisis of each of Erikson's eight psychosocial stages of development. (C,AP)

9. According to Erikson, identity formation is the crisis of adolescence. The adolescent must integrate the self-perceptions and aspirations acquired up to that point. Analyze the difficulties often encountered during this stage. (C,AN)

_____

_____

_____

Social-Learning Theories

Behavioral psychologists view personality development as a set of learned responses. In other words, you are the way you are because your social environment conditioned you to be that way. Social-learning theories combine the principles of behaviorism with those of cognitive psychology. They are based upon the assumption that the individual and the social environment interact. We react to the environment as we perceive it, not necessarily to the way it really is (as pure behaviorists believe). Social-learning theorists believe that as we mature we can to some extent shape our environment to suit our needs.

Social-learning theorists view abnormal behavior as the result of abnormal thoughts. Since these thoughts were learned, the way to cure the behavior is to reshape these "cognitions."

Behaviorism: B.F. Skinner

Although B.F. Skinner did not develop a theory of personality development, his principles of behavior had a great deal of influence upon what would become known as the social-learning theory of development. He demonstrated that animals are sensitive to the consequences of their actions. An individual's actions, therefore, are under the control of external, measurable influences. When an individual receives positive feedback as a result of a particular action, he will continue to act in a similar way. If he receives negative feedback, he will change his actions. According to Skinner, innate reflexes are also subject to modification; therefore, genetic factors are of little importance as determinants of personality. The most important factor of personality development is the way in which the particular society trains its youngsters.

10. Behaviorists, such as B.F. Skinner, believe that one learns from direct experience. Social-learning theorists believe that one also uses vicarious learning to acquire knowledge. Explain what is meant by vicarious learning. Cite an example of something you learned vicariously. (C,AP)

___

___

___

11. Analyze and evaluate this statement made by B.F. Skinner: "Behavior is determined by its consequences." (C,AN,E)

___

___

___

___

Observational Learning: Albert Bandura

Social-learning theorist Albert Bandura proposed that observation and imitation are the most important influences upon social learning. We see others behave in certain ways and observe whether the actions are rewarded or punished. We then try to imitate those behaviors which are positively reinforced and we try to avoid those which are punished. He called this "observational learning."

The basic goal of therapy in observational learning is to help the client choose a more adaptive role and to help the client learn how to play the role. One of the techniques Bandura advocated was modeling. In modeling the therapist demonstrates the desired behavior pattern in a step-by-step manner. The client observes the model's actions and the consequences of those actions.

One of Bandura's most famous experiments involved the attempt to help clients overcome their fear of snakes. It involved the use of modeling and observational learning. First the clients observed as the therapist played with a snake. Then the therapist encouraged them, step-by-step, to approach, touch and, finally, handle the snakes themselves. The experiment was very successful! When completed, all of the subjects had lost their snake phobias!

12. Write a letter to the president of a TV network about your concern that children may use a certain TV character as a model. (C,AP,AN,S,E)

Dear President,

_____
_____
_____
_____
_____
_____
_____

Sincerely,

_____

Humanistic Theories

Humanistic theorists conceive of humans as being above other organisms in that they have some control over their destinies. Humanistic psychologists emphasize our drive for self-actualization, or the tendency to make the most out of our own unique potential. They believe that every individual is motivated to improve himself.

Non-directive Approach: Carl R. Rogers

Carl Rogers suggests that we are all born with a set of experiences, which he calls our phenomenal field. It includes all of our sensory impressions, biological processes and motor outputs. At birth, our phenomenal field is confusing to us, but as time goes on the external world gradually imposes a kind of logic, or order, to it. The more we become aware of this order, the easier it becomes to distinguish our "self" from the rest.

According to Rogers our "self" has an innate desire to reach its full potential. As we mature, our "self" makes more and more judgments (values) about how it should function. Some of these value judgments result from our own desires and some are imposed upon us from the outside world - the society in which we live. An individual encounters problems when society's desires conflict with the self's values. If you must yield too often to society's desires at the expense of your values, your self-concept suffers.

When a situation threatens to worsen your self-concept, you tend to keep the event at the unconscious level. If your own behaviors threaten your self-concept, you may try to keep them, too, from entering your consciousness. In order to achieve self-actualization, however, you must be able to accept yourself completely - faults and virtues alike.

13. Evaluate this statement made by Rogers: "Effective counseling consists of a definitely structured permissive relationship which allows the client to gain an understanding of himself to a degree which enables him to take positive steps in the light of his new orientation." (C,AN,E)

_____
_____
_____
_____

Self-Actualization: Abraham Maslow

Unlike many other theorists, Abraham Maslow based his theories upon the study of highly creative, psychologically healthy individuals. Freud, Jung, Adler, Erikson and Rogers all based their work to a great extent upon the study of abnormal behavior.

Maslow asserted that every individual has certain inherent potentialities that strive for actualization, or full expression. In order for self-actualization to occur, other, more basic needs must first be satisfied; however, these basic needs are not the most important forces in personality development.

Maslow arranged our needs in a hierarchy. Our physiological needs, such as thirst and hunger are the most basic. They must be satisfied before the individual can attend to higher needs, such as security, affection and self-esteem. These needs must also be fulfilled before the individual can strive towards the highest goals, which Maslow referred to as "meta needs." They include such needs as goodness, justice, and unity. When meta needs have been met, the individual has reached a state of self-actualization.

14. Write a character sketch to describe someone who has reached self-actualization. (AN,E)

Social Psychology: The Individual In Society

Social psychology is the study of how individuals behave in their cultural and social environments. Social behaviors and attitudes are influenced by both innate biological and environmental factors. Socialization, or the process of learning from a culture, is also dependent in part upon biological factors.

Morality

What is considered moral must be viewed in the context of a particular culture at a certain time. Even within a culture there are bound to be variations among what is deemed moral.

Many psychologists believe that moral judgment, or the ability to discriminate between good and evil, develops gradually. Young children tend to focus upon the physical consequences of a behavior without considering the intentions of the individual. They tend to think of rules as absolute; they see everything as right or wrong. Many use the degree of punishment to determine the severity of the crime; they judge anyone who is punished as being guilty of a wrongdoing. As a child matures, he begins to realize that rules are not always perfect and that they sometimes conflict with one another. A more mature child takes into account the spirit of the law as well as the letter of the law.

Although moral judgment is an important determinant of moral behavior, it is not the only one. Some individuals are able to make mature judgments as to what is good and evil but lack the self-control or courage to act accordingly. When an individual consistently acts in accordance with the rules of society, we say that the rules have been internalized and that the individual has been socialized.

1. Studies have shown that children raised by nurturant adults who follow a love-oriented approach to discipline are more likely to internalize moral controls. Analyze the reasons. (AN,E)

_____
_____
_____
_____
_____

Social Attitudes

An attitude is a consistent way of thinking and feeling about an aspect of our social environment. The beliefs (or belief) upon which an attitude is based may consist of factual information. On the other hand, they may consist of generalizations, stereotypes, rationalizations and so on. In a similar fashion, the emotional element of an attitude may be based upon actual, relevant experiences or it may result from second-hand or even irrelevant experiences with the object. There are many factors which interact to influence the formation of our attitudes. Three of the main determinants of an individual's attitudes are family influences, peer influences and the individual's personality. Although there is a tendency with to behave according to our attitudes, our behavior is sometimes inconsistent with our beliefs and feelings.

2. One of the ways in which parents influence their children's attitudes is by exposing them to their own attitudes and life style. Those that also encourage their children to learn about opposing viewpoints and attitudes, however, actually reinforce their own ideas. Analyze the reasons this is so. (AN)

_____
_____
_____
_____

3. A primitive belief is one that is accepted on authority rather than being derived from supporting premises. Higher-order beliefs are based upon supporting premises. In time, however, they may become primitive beliefs. Higher-order beliefs are more vulnerable to change. Under what circumstances would the individual be least likely to change a higher-order belief? (C,AN)

_____
_____
_____
_____

Persuasion and Attitude Change

We are constantly exposed to pressures to change our beliefs and attitudes. The effectiveness of this persuasion depends a great deal upon the <u>communicator</u>, or person trying to induce the change, and the nature of the <u>message</u> being communicated. You are more likely to accept a message from a communicator whom you perceive to hold similar attitudes as you. A credible communicator, one whom you believe to be trustworthy, is usually more effective than one perceived as untrustworthy. An interesting phenomenon, however, is the so-called "sleeper effect." Psychologists Carl I. Hovland and Walter Weiss studied the influence of credibility on attitude change. They found that after a period of time the audience (the person or persons whose attitude the communicator wishes to change) forgets the source and remembers only the information.

The way the message is presented also has an effect on how influenced the audience will be. It is most likely to influence a change in the audience if the intent to persuade is disguised. Balanced presentations are more effective than one-sided ones, especially if the audience's points of view are presented first.

Even when the communicator is highly credible and even when the message is well-constructed to fit the situation and the audience, many individuals are resistant to attitude change. Whether or not others in the individual's social group accept the information has a great impact upon the individual's acceptance or rejection of the information. If the groups with which the individual affiliates share an attitude, the individual is likely to resist any change. Personality factors also have an effect upon resistance to change; highly-anxious, self-defensive personalities seem to be less inclined to give in to persuasion.

4. Suppose you had a product to sell and wanted to advertize on T.V. If you had your choice of anyone in the world to serve as your communicator, whom would you choose? Why? (C,AN,E)

_____

_____

_____

5. In order to counteract views which oppose our own, we sometimes distort and exaggerate the opposing viewpoint to make it seem less credible. Write a speech which exaggerates a view to which you are opposed. (C,AP,AN,E,S)

Evidence suggests that although fear-arousing messages are effective in evoking emotional responses, they are not as effective in changing attitudes or in protecting the audience from counter-propaganda as are minimal-fear messages.

6. Design 2 posters to change smokers' attitudes towards cigarettes: one with a high-fear message and the other with a minimal-fear message. (C,AP,AN,E,S)

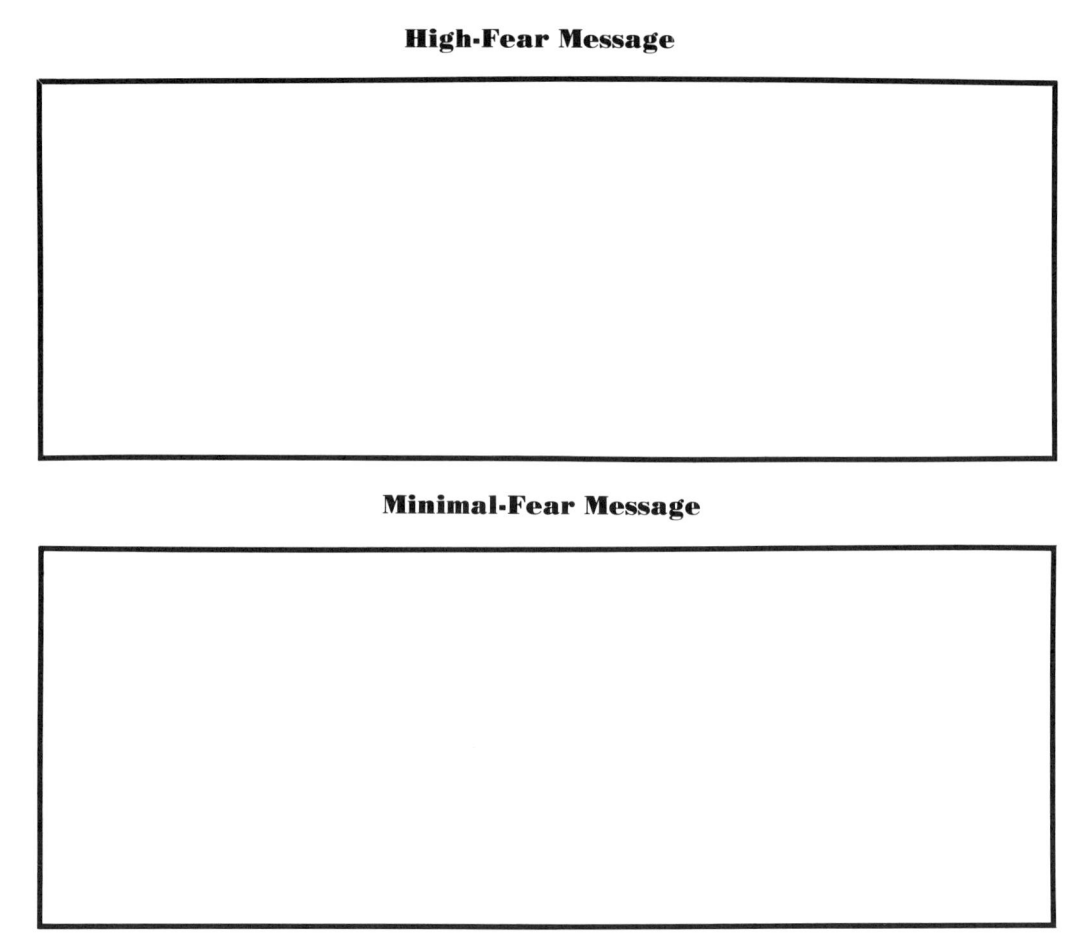

High-Fear Message

Minimal-Fear Message

Person Perception

We form impressions of people according to principles similar to those followed in perceiving other objects in our environment. When we don't have complete information about an individual, we tend to fill in the missing data according to our expectations. We obtain the data from a number of sources. One of the most important sources is our own implicit theory of personality. In other words, we already have a personal theory of which traits tend to go with one another; when we know one trait, we add others which, according to our implicit theory, seem to go with that trait. Other important influences upon person perception are our stereotypes. We often perceive an individual in terms of the person's group membership. Our perceptions of the individual are often based upon those stereotyped impressions rather than upon the individual's personal attributes. The halo effect is a similar type of influence. It involves our general grouping of people into the "good" and the "bad." If our main impression of a person is favorable, we tend to attribute many different kinds of favorable traits to that individual. In a similar fashion, if our general evaluation of an individual is unfavorable, we tend to attribute to him all sorts of unfavorable traits!

Other factors play a role in impression formation. The order in which we receive information is also important. First impressions tend to dominate our later handling of additional information about an individual. This is known as the primary effect. Even when the initial information is merely a list of descriptive adjectives, the earlier descriptions tend to be retained by the perceiver to a greater degree than words presented at the end of the list.

G. Heider and other social psychologists proposed a set of principles which has become known as the balance theory. It is based upon the assumption that people seek harmonious relations. In order to maintain harmony, or balance, we tend to view relations according to certain rules: (1) We expect people we like to like each other; (2) we expect to like a person disliked by someone we dislike; and (3) we expect to like a person liked by someone we like. Sometimes we find ourselves in a disharmonious, or unbalanced, relation. It causes us to be quite uncomfortable.

We also form impressions about a person's intentions and motives. The main distinction we make is whether a behavior is intentional, accidental or externally caused. Of these, only intentional behavior should influence one's perception of the individual's personality. Of course, just as our other means of perceiving a person's personality are often misleading, so is our interpretation of motives.

7. When a person's true characteristics conflict with the perceiver's image of the person's group, the perceiver resists having to change his group stereotype. What might the perceiver do to avoid the need to modify his stereotype? (C,AN,E)

_____

_____

_____

8. Which would make you more uncomfortable: being liked by someone you dislike or being disliked by someone you dislike? Why? (C,AN)

_____

_____

_____

9. Evaluate this statement in terms of personal experience: We attribute our own inappropriate behavior to the environment and the inappropriate behavior of others to their personality. (C,AN,E)

_____

_____

_____

Social Groups

Beginning at birth and continuing throughout our lives we belong to many groups. The first groups we belong to are those into which we are born: family and ethnic groups. Some of the groups we join are formal groups with a definite set of rules. Others are informal; although they do not have a formal set of rules, they, too, have rules governing the behavior of the members. Rules in an informal group are based upon the cultural expectations of the members.

To be considered a group, a set of persons should have certain characteristics. First of all, the persons should perceive themselves as a group. They should share some goals and believe that the group will serve to fulfill some of their needs. Members of a group should interact with one another according to their status within the group. If several persons are grouped together but do not have the characteristics of a group, we call the set of persons an aggregate.

10. Draw a series of pictures that illustrates a situation in which an aggregate might become a group. (C,AP,AN,S)

11. Bystander apathy is a phenomenon of aggregates. Studies indicate that a lone individual is more apt to assist a stranger than if he were one of several bystanders. Analyze the reasons for this phenomenon. (AN)

_____

_____

_____

12. Groups tend to act in riskier, less responsible ways than would individuals acting alone. Describe an incident in which you (or someone you know) behaved in a way that you would not have behaved if alone. (AP,AN)

_____

_____

_____

Conformity

There are two general kinds of social influence: informational and normative. <u>Informational influence</u> is the tendency to accept information provided by others as evidence of reality even when it conflicts with evidence received by our own senses. <u>Normative influence</u> is the tendency to modify our behavior to conform with what is perceived as the behavior expected by the group.

As far back as 1935 social psychologist Muzafer Sherif first conducted experiments to test the affects of informational influence upon subjects. He used the auto-kinetic effect as the basis for his studies. The auto-kinetic effect is the phenomenon in which a stationary pinpoint of light in an otherwise dark room seems to move. Because the apparent movement is created by the movement of the individual's eyes and not any real movement of the light, the distance the light appears to move varies from person to person. The subjects in the experiment were told the study was on visual perception. While the subjects were in the waiting room, they "overheard" the judgments of stooges who had been hired by the experimenters. About 2/3 of Sherif's subjects were greatly influenced by the prior measurements given by the stooges!

In the 1960's Stanley Milgram performed a set of experiments which placed his subjects in an extremely stressful situation. The subjects believed they were part of an experiment to study the effects of punishment upon learning. Each was to act like a teacher; every time the "subject" (who was, in fact, a stooge) made a mistake, the "teacher" was to administer a shock. The machine with which the shock was to be administered was also a fake. For each mistake, the teacher was told to increase the intensity of the shock. Milgram instructed the "teacher" that he must go on until the subject made no mistakes. Even when the stooge pretended to have suffered an attack, the "teacher" was instructed to continue. Out of the first 40 subjects in Milgram's experiments, about 65 percent continued right to the end, although they were extremely distressed about the situation.

13. Milgram's experiments provided a measure of the subjects' willingness to engage in antisocial acts when under great social pressure to do so. How do you think you would have reacted if you had been one of Milgram's subjects? At what point do you think you would have chosen to disobey the experimenter? (AN,E)

_____

_____

_____

In 1956 S. Asch performed a set of experiments to study how an individual would respond in a judgmental situation if he believed his perceptions to be correct, but others in the group contradicted him. In these experiments all but one out of 3 to 10 in the group were told in advance to respond incorrectly to a question involving the size of 3 lines. The real subject went last. About 1/3 of the real subjects conformed to the group even when the correct answer was obvious. Whether or not the subject answered according to his own views was dependent upon several factors. The more people in the group, the more likely the subject was to conform; however, if even one member was added who agreed with the subject, the subject resisted group pressure and responded according to his perceptions. Another factor was the stimulus itself. If the correct answer and the one given by the group were close in size, the more likely the individual was to conform.

14. About 2/3 of Asch's subjects resisted conformity. Analyze the aspects of a person's personality that would enable him to withstand group pressure. (AN,E)

_____

_____

_____

Personal Space

Personal space refers to the space surrounding one's body that the person considers private. The amount of personal space that is preferred varies from culture to culture and from situation to situation.

15. Observe the physical distances people seek in a variety of settings: a library, an elevator, a bus, a coffee shop counter, a cafeteria, etc. What kinds of things do people do in crowded situations in order to decrease their feelings of invasion? Do acquaintances stand closer than strangers when conversing? Report on your observations. (C,AP,AN)

Leadership

Studies done by sociologist Robert Bales and others have indicated that there are two types of leaders: task specialists and social-emotional specialists. The task specialist often gives opinions and makes suggestions. This type of leader frequently reminds the group of its goals and helps keep members on track. The social-emotional specialist uses praise and other positive feedback to maintain group solidarity. This type of leader often asks for suggestions rather than give them.

16. Think about a group of which you are a member. Who is a task specialist? Who is a social-emotional specialist? Do you know anyone who is an expert at carrying out both leadership roles?

_____

_____

_____